COLLINS

First
DICTIONARY

Ginny Lapage

Collins

A Division of HarperCollins*Publishers*

HarperCollins Children's Books
A Division of HarperCollins Publishers Ltd
77-85 Fulham Palace Road
Hammersmith
London W6 8JB

First published in 1995 in the United Kingdom
by HarperCollins Publishers Ltd as *Collins First Dictionary*

ISBN: 0 00 197001-1

A CIP record for this book is available from the British Library

Printed and bound in Italy

Text: Ginny Lapage
Illustrations: John Rogan, Georgien Overwater (Maggie Mundy Illustrator's Agency),
Anthony Lewis (Peters, Fraser & Dunlop), Sumiko Davies (Peters, Fraser & Dunlop),
Jean Bayliss (Elizabeth Roy Literary Agency), Peter Utton (Graham-Cameron Illustration)

Art Editor: Susi Martin
Designer: Jacqueline Palmer
Editor: Sarah Allen

NOTE TO PARENTS AND TEACHERS

The *Collins First Dictionary* has been written and designed for children who are starting to learn reading and writing skills. The 2,000 headwords have been carefully selected and defined on the basis of classroom research. The definitions are clear, simple and friendly. Examples (shown in italics) are used where they help to clarify the definition.

Each page is illustrated with lively and amusing pictures to help motivate young children to look, read and learn. A full alphabet at the bottom of each double page shows children how to write capital and small letters.

The dictionary has been thoughtfully set out to help children learn some simple grammar:

NOUNS
Where the headword is a noun (e.g. **man**), the plural is given in brackets, e.g.:

man (men)

ADJECTIVES
Where the headword is an adjective (e.g. **good**), the comparative and superlative forms are given in brackets, e.g.:

good (better, best)

VERBS
Where the headword is a verb (e.g. **go**), parts of the verb are given in brackets. The verb parts given are: the 3rd person present tense (goes), the present participle (going), the past tense (went) and the past participle (gone). However, if the past tense and the past participle are identical, only one form is given, e.g.:

run (runs, running, ran)

WORDS WITH MORE THAN ONE MEANING
Where a word has more than one meaning, the definitions are separated and numbered, e.g.:

bat (bats)
1. A bat is a small animal like a mouse with wings.
2. A bat is a piece of wood you use for hitting a ball in a game.

WORDS WITH MORE THAN ONE FUNCTION
Where a word has more than one function, i.e. the word is a noun *and* a verb, or a noun *and* an adjective, the headword is repeated and numbered for each of the different functions, e.g.:

cold ¹ (colds)
A cold is an illness that makes you sneeze and your nose run.

cold ² (colder, coldest)
When the weather is cold, the temperature is low outside.

The *Collins First Dictionary* is designed to combine pleasure and learning!

accident (accidents)
If you have an accident, something nasty happens to you when you do not expect it.
The accident happened when he slipped off the ladder.

act (acts, acting, acted)
If you act in a play, you pretend to be someone else.
He acted as the prince in the Christmas play.

actor (actors)
An actor is a person who performs in a play or film.

add (adds, adding, added)
1. When you add something, you put it with something else.
2. When you add numbers together, you find out how many there are altogether.
If you add six and two, the number you get is eight.

address (addresses)
Your address tells people exactly where you live. It is the name or number of your house, the street, town and postcode.

adult (adults)
An adult is a grown-up person.

adventure (adventures)
You have an adventure when you do something exciting and sometimes dangerous.
My adventure began when I took the wrong turning in the woods.

aeroplane (aeroplanes)
An aeroplane is a machine that flies in the air.

afraid
If you are afraid, you are scared or worried that something may hurt you.
The mouse was afraid to come out of its hole.

afternoon (afternoons)
The afternoon is the time between lunch and evening.

again
If you do something again, you do it after you have done it once already.

4

Aa Bb Cc Dd Ee Ff Gg Hh Ii Jj Kk Ll Mm

A

against
If you lean against something, you rest your body on it.

ago
Something that happened long ago happened a long time before now.
Long, long ago there lived an ugly troll.

age (ages)
Your age is how old you are.

agree (agrees, agreeing, agreed)
If you agree with something or someone, you think the same way as they do.

air
Air is all around you but you cannot see it. You need air to breathe.

airport (airports)
An airport is a place where aircraft take off and land.

alarm (alarms)
1. An alarm is a signal that warns you of danger.
The fire alarm went off and the children left the building.
2. An alarm is a sound that wakes you up in the morning.

alien (aliens)
An alien is a creature that comes from another planet.

alive
If something is alive, it is living, not dead.

alligator (alligators)
An alligator is a large reptile like a crocodile. Alligators live in lakes and rivers in America and China.

allow (allows, allowing, allowed)
If you allow someone to do something, you let them do it.
My mum will allow me to play at your house when I've put my clothes away.

almost
If you almost do something, you nearly do it.
I almost finished making my model when I ran out of glue.

alone
If you are alone, you are by yourself.

alphabet (alphabets)
An alphabet is all the letters that are used in writing, arranged in a special order.

5

Nn Oo Pp Qq Rr Ss Tt Uu Vv Ww Xx Yy Zz

always

Always means every time.
It always rains when I go on holiday.

ambulance (ambulances)

An ambulance is a van for taking people to hospital. It often has a flashing light on top.

amphibian (amphibians)

Amphibians are animals that live in water when they begin life and live on land when they become adults. Toads are amphibians.

ancient

Something that is ancient is very, very old.
There was an ancient tree at the end of our garden.

angry

If you are angry, you feel upset and cross with someone or something.
She was so angry that she stamped her foot and made a hole in the floor.

animal (animals)

An animal is anything that is living and can move.

ankle (ankles)

Your ankle is the joint between your leg and your foot.

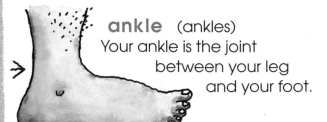

annoy (annoys, annoying, annoyed)

If you annoy someone, you make them cross by doing something they don't like.
My sister annoys me when she plays her music very loudly.

answer (answers, answering, answered)

When someone asks you a question, you answer them by saying something back.

ant (ants)

An ant is a tiny insect that lives in a large group called a colony.

antelope (antelopes)

An antelope is an animal that looks like a deer. It has horns and can run very fast. Antelopes live in Africa and Asia.

anxious

If you are anxious, you feel worried about something.

apartment (apartments)

An apartment is a group of rooms where people live on one floor of a large building.
The skyscraper had three apartments on each floor.

6

Aa Bb Cc Dd Ee Ff Gg Hh Ii Jj Kk Ll Mm

ape (apes)
An ape is an animal like a large monkey with no tail. Chimpanzees, orang-utans and gibbons are all apes.

appear (appears, appearing, appeared)
If you appear, you can be seen after not being seen.
The woman suddenly appeared from behind the door.

appetite (appetites)
If you have an appetite, you are always ready to eat at mealtimes.

apple (apples)
An apple is a round red, yellow or green fruit that grows on a tree. It is usually crisp and has pips. You can eat it raw or cooked.

April
April is the fourth month of the year. It has 30 days.

arch (arches)
An arch is a curved shape in a building. It is often used over a window or a doorway.
She looked through the arch of the window and saw the sheep grazing in the field.

area (areas)
1. The area of something flat is its size.
2. If you talk about an area of a country, you mean a part of it.
There was a beautiful area of woodland beside the river.

argue (argues, arguing, argued)
When you argue with someone, you talk about things that you do not agree about.
I argued with my mum because I did not want to wear my woolly hat.

arm (arms)
Your arm is the part of your body between your shoulder and your hand.

armour
Armour is special clothing, usually made of metal, that is worn to cover the body when fighting.
The knight's armour shone in the sun as he waited to fight the dragon.

arrive (arrives, arriving, arrived)
When you arrive somewhere, you get to the end of your journey.

7

Nn Oo Pp Qq Rr Ss Tt Uu Vv Ww Xx Yy Zz

ask (asks, asking, asked)
If you ask someone something, you want to know the answer to a question.
'Why can't you see stars in the daytime?' he asked.

asleep
When you are asleep, your eyes are closed and you are not awake.

assistant (assistants)
An assistant is someone who helps other people to do something.
The shop assistant asked if I needed help to find the book I wanted.

8

ate   See **eat**

attack (attacks, attacking, attacked)
If something attacks you, it tries to hurt you suddenly.
The wasps attacked Katy when she trod on their nest.

attention
1. If you pay attention to someone, you listen carefully to what they are saying.
2. If someone or something attracts your attention, you notice them.
The boys in the boat waved their arms to attract attention.

August
August is the eighth month of the year. It has 31 days.

aunt (aunts)
Your aunt is the sister of your mother or father.

autumn
Autumn is the season after summer and before winter, when leaves fall off the trees.

awake
When you are awake, you are not sleeping.
I was so excited about going to the fair that I stayed awake all night.

awful
If something is awful, it is very bad or nasty.

Jonathan made an awful mess in the kitchen.

axe (axes)
An axe is a weapon with a long handle and a heavy blade at one end. It is used for chopping wood.

Aa Bb Cc Dd Ee Ff Gg Hh Ii Jj Kk Ll Mm

B

baby (babies)
A baby is a new-born child.

back (backs)
1. Your back is the part of your body between your neck and your bottom.
2. The back of something is opposite the front.

bacon
Bacon is the salted meat which comes from a pig.
He liked eggs and bacon for breakfast.

bad (worse, worst)
1. If you are bad, you are naughty.
2. If food is bad, you cannot eat it.

badger (badgers)
A badger is a large grey animal with black stripes on its face. It lives in an underground tunnel called a set.

bag (bags)
A bag is for carrying things in. It is open at the top and can be made of paper, leather, cloth or plastic.

bake (bakes, baking, baked)
If you bake something, you cook it in an oven.
I helped my gran bake some biscuits.

balance (balances, balancing, balanced)
When you balance something, you keep it steady.

ball (balls)
A ball is a round object that you use to play games with.

balloon (balloons)
A balloon is a small, brightly-coloured bag made of thin rubber. When you blow air into it, it gets bigger.

banana (bananas)
A banana is a long-curved fruit with a thick yellow skin.

band (bands)
A band is a group of people who play musical instruments together.

9

bandage (bandages)
A bandage is a strip of material that you use to wrap around a cut.

banish (banishes, banishing, banished)
If you banish someone, you send them away from the land where they live to punish them.
The king's enemies were banished to a deserted island.

bank (banks)
1. A bank is a place that looks after money and other valuable things.
2. A bank is the ground at the edge of a river or a stream.

bar (bars)
A bar is a long thin piece of wood or metal.

bark[1] (barks)
Bark is the hard covering on the trunk and branches of a tree.

bark[2] (barks, barking, barked)
When a dog barks, it makes a short loud sound.

basket (baskets)
A basket is a bag made of cane or thin strips of wood. It is open at the top and is used for carrying and holding things in.
She carried all her eggs in a round basket.

bat (bats)
1. A bat is a small animal like a mouse with wings.
2. A bat is a piece of wood you use for hitting a ball in a game.

bath (baths)
A bath is a large container that you fill with water to wash yourself in.

battle (battles)
A battle is a fight in a war between ships, armies or aeroplanes.

battery (batteries)
A battery has electricity inside it. You use batteries to make things work.
My watch stopped working when the battery ran out.

beach (beaches)
A beach is the land at the edge of the sea. It is usually covered with sand or pebbles.
We made shell pictures on the beach.

beak (beaks)
A beak is the hard pointed part of a bird's mouth.

bean (beans)
A bean is a vegetable. The outside is called a pod. Seeds grow on the inside, and are also called beans.

10

Aa Bb Cc Dd Ee Ff Gg Hh Ii Jj Kk Ll Mm

bear (bears)
A bear is a large strong wild animal with thick fur and sharp claws. Bears usually live in caves in cool countries and some can be very dangerous.

beard (beards)
A beard is the hair that grows on a man's chin.

beautiful
If someone or something is beautiful, they are very pretty or attractive to look at.

bed (beds)
A bed is a piece of furniture to rest or sleep on.

bee (bees)
A bee is a small flying insect with black and yellow stripes that can sting. Bees are important to flowers and fruit trees because they spread pollen between them.
Bees make honey.

beetle (beetles)
A beetle is an insect with hard wing covers.

begin (begins, beginning, began, begun)
When you begin something, you start to do it.

behave (behaves, behaving, behaved)
The way you behave is how you do things. *Tom's mother was cross because he behaved badly at the party.*

behind
If something is behind, it is at the back of something. *William found his football hidden behind the greenhouse.*

believe (believes, believing, believed)
If you believe something, you are sure that it is true.

bell (bells)
1. A bell is a hollow piece of metal shaped like a cup which rings when you strike it.
2. A bell is a button on a door that you press to make it ring indoors.

belong (belongs, belonging, belonged)
1. If you belong to something like a club, you are a member of it.
2. If something belongs to you, it is yours.

This bag belongs to Emma Jones

This book belongs to Emma Jones

11

Nn Oo Pp Qq Rr Ss Tt Uu Vv Ww Xx Yy Zz

bend (bends, bending, bent)
If you bend something, you stop it being straight.
I bent my plastic ruler and it snapped in half!

best
Something or somebody that is the best is better than any of the others.

better
1. If you can do something better than someone else, you are cleverer than they are at it.
2. If you are better, you are well again.

bicycle (bicycles)
A bicycle is a machine with two wheels that you ride by pressing down on the pedals. A bicycle is also called a bike.

big (bigger, biggest)
If something is big it is large.

bin (bins)
A bin is a container to put things in.

bird (birds)
A bird is a creature with wings, feathers and a beak. Most birds can fly. The young are hatched from eggs.

birthday (birthdays)
Your birthday is special because it is the day of the year that you were born.

biscuit (biscuits)
A biscuit is a crisp thin cake.

bite (bites, biting, bit, bitten)
When you bite something, you cut it with your teeth.
The dog bit the burglar as he tried to escape.

black (blacker, blackest)
Black is the colour of coal.

blackbird (blackbirds)
A blackbird is a common wild bird with a beautiful song. The male has black feathers and a yellow beak and the female has brown feathers.

blade (blades)
A blade is the sharp edge of a knife.

blame (blames, blaming, blamed)
If you blame someone for doing something, you think they did it.
We blamed Timmy the cat for eating our supper.

12

Aa Bb Cc Dd Ee Ff Gg Hh Ii Jj Kk Ll Mm

B

blanket (blankets)
A blanket is a warm cover on a bed.

blew See **blow**

blind[1] (blinds)
A blind is a rolled piece of material that you pull down to cover a window.

blind[2]
Someone who is blind cannot see.

block[1] (blocks)
1. A block of flats or offices is a tall building where many people live or work.
2. A block is a big piece of stone, wood or metal.

block[2] (blocks, blocking, blocked)
If you block something, you stop anything getting through it.
The sink was blocked so the water overflowed.

blood
Blood is the red liquid that your heart pumps around inside your body.

blow (blows, blowing, blew, blown)
1. When you blow, you push air out of your mouth.
2. When the wind blows, the air moves.
The wind was blowing so hard that I nearly fell off my bike.

blue (bluer, bluest)
Blue is the colour of the sky.

boat (boats)
A boat is a small ship that floats. Boats take people and goods across rivers or the sea.

body (bodies)
Your body is the whole of you.

boil (boils, boiling, boiled)
If you boil water or milk, you heat it until it bubbles and steams.

bone (bones)
Bones are the hard parts inside your body. Together they form your skeleton.

bonfire (bonfires)
A bonfire is a large fire that is lit outdoors.

book (books)
A book is made of pages of paper fixed together inside a cover.

13

Nn Oo Pp Qq Rr Ss Tt Uu Vv Ww Xx Yy Zz

boot (boots)
1. Boots are a kind of shoe. People wear boots to cover their feet and ankles.
2. The boot of a car is the place where you put your luggage.

bored
If you are bored, you feel tired and cross because you have nothing interesting to do.

born
When a baby is born, it comes out of its mother's body and begins its own life.

borrow (borrows, borrowing, borrowed)
When you borrow something from someone, they let you have it for a short time.

14

bottle (bottles)
A bottle is a tall glass or plastic container which is used to hold liquids.

bottom (bottoms)
The bottom of something is the lowest part.

bought See **buy**

bounce (bounces, bouncing, bounced)
If you bounce a ball, you hit it against something hard and it springs back.

bowl (bowls)
A bowl is a round deep dish made for holding things like soup, cereals and puddings.

box (boxes)
A box is a container with a lid. It is usually made from cardboard, wood or plastic.

boy (boys)
A boy is a male child.

branch (branches)
A branch is a part of a tree that grows out from its trunk.

brave (braver, bravest)
If you are brave, you are not afraid of danger.
The dog was so brave that it jumped into the river to rescue the baby.

bread
Bread is a food made of flour, water and, usually, yeast.

break (breaks, breaking, broke, broken)
If you break something, it splits into pieces or stops working.

Aa Bb Cc Dd Ee Ff Gg Hh Ii Jj Kk Ll Mm

breakfast (breakfasts)
Breakfast is the first meal of the day. You have breakfast when you get up in the morning.

breathe (breathes, breathing, breathed)
When you breathe, you take air in and out of your body through your nose or mouth.

brick (bricks)
A brick is a small rectangular block of baked clay. Bricks are used for building.

bridge (bridges)
A bridge is a path or road built to go over a river, railway or road so that people can cross safely.

bright (brighter, brightest)
1. If a light is bright, it shines strongly.
2. A person who is bright is clever.

bring
(brings, bringing, brought)
If you bring something to a place, you carry it with you.
Bring a bag to put the shopping in.

broke See **break**

broken See **break**

broom (brooms)
A broom is a brush with a long handle. You can use it to sweep the floor or a path.

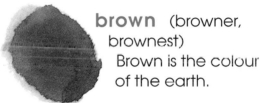

brother (brothers)
Your brother is a boy who has the same mother and father as you

brought See **bring**

brown (browner, brownest)
Brown is the colour of the earth.

15

brush (brushes)
A brush is made of wood, plastic or metal with lots of short stiff hairs fixed to it. You use brushes for painting, for cleaning things and for brushing your hair and teeth.

bubble (bubbles)
A bubble is a shiny ball of soapy liquid with air inside.

bucket (buckets)
A bucket is a container with a handle. Buckets are used for carrying liquid.

build (builds, building, built)
If you build something, you make it by joining the parts together.

Nn Oo Pp Qq Rr Ss Tt Uu Vv Ww Xx Yy Zz

building (buildings)
A building has walls and a roof. For example, a house, a school, a church and a factory are buildings.

built See **build**

bulb (bulbs)
1. A bulb is the root of some flowers. *Grandpa bought daffodil and snowdrop bulbs for the garden.*
2. A bulb is the part of a lamp that gives light.

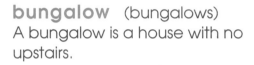

bungalow (bungalows)
A bungalow is a house with no upstairs.

burger (burgers)
A burger is a bun filled with a flat round piece of minced beef.

burglar (burglars)
A burglar is someone who breaks into houses and steals things.

burn (burns, burning, burned)
1. If something burns, it is on fire.
2. If something hot burns you, it hurts you with the heat.

burst (bursts, bursting, burst)
If something bursts, it splits open suddenly.

bus (buses)
A bus is a large vehicle for taking lots of people from one place to another.

bush (bushes)
A bush is a small woody plant with lots of branches.

busy busier, busiest)
1. If you are busy, you have a lot to do.
2. A busy place has a lot going on in it.

butterfly (butterflies)
A butterfly is an insect with four large wings. It begins life as an egg, hatches out into a caterpillar, then spins a cocoon around itself and later comes out as a butterfly.

button (buttons)
Buttons are sewn onto clothes to hold them together.

buy (buys, buying, bought)
If you buy something, you pay money to get it.
I bought some string for my kite with my birthday money.

buzz (buzzes, buzzing, buzzed)
If something buzzes, it makes a sound like a bee.

16

Aa Bb Cc Dd Ee Ff Gg Hh Ii Jj Kk Ll Mm

cabbage
(cabbages)
A cabbage is a round leafy vegetable. They are usually green, but they can also be red or white.

cage (cages)
A cage is a box with bars for keeping pets such as hamsters, mice and budgerigars.

cake (cakes)
A cake is a sweet food usually made from eggs, flour, sugar and butter. It is baked in an oven.

calculator (calculators)
A calculator is a machine that you use to help you to do sums.
I got all my number work right because I used my calculator.

calendar (calendars)
A calendar is a list which shows all the days of the week and the months of the year.

call (calls, calling, called)
1. If you call someone, you speak loudly to tell them to come to you.
2. If you call a person or a thing something, you give them a name.

camel (camels)
A camel is a large animal with one or two humps on its back. Camels are used instead of horses in the desert because they can travel long distances without eating or drinking.

camera (cameras)
You use a camera to take photos.

camp (camps)
A camp is a place where people live for a short time. They may use tents, huts or a caravan for shelter.

camping
If you go camping, you go on holiday to stay in a tent.
We went camping in France last year.

candle
(candles)
A candle is a stick of wax with a piece of string through the middle. When you light the string, the wax burns slowly and the flame gives light.

car (cars)
A car has four wheels and an engine to make it go. You can travel on the road in a car.

17

Nn Oo Pp Qq Rr Ss Tt Uu Vv Ww Xx Yy Zz

caravan (caravans)
A caravan is a home on wheels. People bring their caravans with them by towing them on the back of their car. *We took our caravan to the seaside for a weekend break.*

card (cards)
1. Card is stiff paper.
2. A card can be used to send a message for a special occasion.

cardboard
Cardboard is very thick strong paper which can be used to make things like boxes.

18

care (cares, caring, cared)
1. If you care about something, you think it is important.
2. If you take care of something, you look after it.

careful
If you are careful, you make sure that you do things in a sensible way.

careless
If you are careless, you do not think about what you are doing.
Pat was so careless that she did not look as she stepped into the road.

carpet (carpets)
A carpet is a cover for the floor. It is usually made of something like wool.

carrot (carrots)
A carrot is a long thin vegetable that is orange in colour.

carry (carries, carrying, carried)
If you carry something, you take it from one place to another.

carton (cartons)
A carton is a cardboard or plastic container used for milk or juice.

cartoon (cartoons)
1. A cartoon is a film made using a series of pictures. Instead of actors, the characters are drawings.
2. A cartoon is a drawing that tells a joke.

case (cases)
A case is a box that you use to carry or keep things in.
My pencil case is full of broken pencils.

cash
Cash is money. It comes in the form of coins and paper notes.

Aa Bb Cc Dd Ee Ff Gg Hh Ii Jj Kk Ll Mm

castle
(castles)
A castle is a big building with thick walls and towers. Castles were built many years ago to keep the people living inside safe from their enemies.

cat (cats)
A cat is an animal that is covered with fur. Small cats are often kept as pets. Large cats like lions and tigers live in the wild.

catch (catches, catching, caught)
1. When you catch something, you take hold of it while it is moving.
2. If you catch an illness, you get it from someone else who has got it.
Mark caught chicken pox from Inge.

caterpillar (caterpillars)
A caterpillar is a small worm-like creature with legs. It changes into a butterfly or a moth.

caught See catch

cave (caves)
A cave is a large hole in a rock or under the ground
They took shelter in the cave when it started to rain.

centre (centres)
The centre of something is the middle of it.

cereal (cereals)
1. Cereals are plants that farmers grow for seed. Oats, barley and wheat are cereals.
2. Cereal is food made from the seed of cereal plants. It is often eaten at breakfast with milk.

ceremony (ceremonies)
A ceremony is a special and important occasion when people gather together.
The wedding ceremony was a very happy event.

chain (chains)
A chain is made of metal rings joined together in a line.

chair (chairs)
A chair is a seat with a back for one person.

chalk (chalks)
1. Chalk is soft white rock.
2. A piece of chalk is a stick of soft white rock that you write with on a chalkboard.

19

Nn Oo Pp Qq Rr Ss Tt Uu Vv Ww Xx Yy Zz

change[1]
Change is the money you get back if you have given more money than is needed to pay for something.

change[2] (changes, changing, changed)
When something changes, it becomes different.

channel (channels)
1. A channel is a narrow stretch of water between two pieces of land.
2. A channel on the television set has its own group of programmes.

charge[1] (charges, charging, charged)
If someone charges you for something, they ask you to pay money for it.
He charged me 25p for two apples.

charge[2]
If you are in charge of something, you are the person that makes sure that it is looked after.
Janie is in charge of the book corner. She keeps it very tidy.

chase (chases, chasing, chased)
When you chase someone or something, you run after them and try to catch them.

cheap (cheaper, cheapest)
Something that is cheap does not cost very much.

checkout (checkouts)
A checkout is the place in a shop where you pay for things.

cheek (cheeks)
Your cheeks are the soft part of your face on each side of your nose and mouth.
Ramin's cheeks went bright red when he was caught cheating.

cheese (cheeses)
Cheese is a food made from milk. There are many kinds of cheeses.

chest (chests)
1. A chest is a large strong box with a lid.
2. Your chest is the top front part of your body between your neck and your waist.

chick (chicks)
A chick is a newborn bird.

chicken (chickens)
A chicken is a young bird which farmers keep. We eat the eggs that chickens lay.

20

child (children)
A child is a young boy or girl.

chin (chins)
Your chin is the part of your face under your mouth.

chip (chips)
A chip is a thin piece of potato which is fried.
We have fish and chips for tea on Friday.

chocolate (chocolates)
Chocolate is a sweet or a drink. It is made from cocoa, milk and sugar. Milk, ice cream and cakes can be flavoured with chocolate.

choose
(chooses, choosing, chose, chosen)
If you choose something, you pick out the one you want.
Choose the video you want now or we won't have one at all!

circle (circles)
A circle is a shape that is perfectly round.

circus
(circuses)
A circus is a show held in a tent called a big top. Acrobats, clowns and jugglers all perform tricks for the people watching.

city (cities)
A city is a very big town. London, Paris and Washington are all cities.

class (classes)
A class is a group of pupils who are taught together in school.

clean¹ (cleans, cleaning, cleaned)
If you clean something, you take the dirt away from it.

clean²
(cleaner, cleanest)
If something is clean, it has no dirty marks on it.

clear¹ (clears, clearing, cleared)
If you clear things away, you tidy up.

21

Nn Oo Pp Qq Rr Ss Tt Uu Vv Ww Xx Yy Zz

clear² (clearer, clearest)
1. If something is clear, it is easy to understand.
2. If something like glass or plastic is clear, you can see through it.

clever (cleverer, cleverest)
If you are clever, you are able to learn to do things very easily.

cliff (cliffs)
A cliff is a steep hill with a side that goes straight down. Most cliffs are next to the sea.

climb (climbs, climbing, climbed)
If you climb a hill or a ladder, you go up it.

cling (clings, clinging, clung)
When you cling to something, you hold on to it tightly.
The baby koala bear clung to its mother.

clinic (clinics)
A clinic is a place where people go to get advice about their health.

cloak (cloaks)
A cloak is a loose coat that has no sleeves.

clock (clocks)
A clock is a machine that shows the time.

close¹ (closes, closing, closed) (rhymes with nose)
If you close something, you shut it.

close² (closer, closest) (rhymes with dose)
Something that is close is near.
They knew they were close to the end of the tunnel because they could see light.

cloth (cloths)
1. Cloth is fabric used for making things like clothes and curtains.
2. A cloth is a piece of fabric used for cleaning things.

clothes
Clothes are the things people wear, such as skirts, trousers, dresses and jumpers.
My favourite clothes are my jogging pants and a sweatshirt.

cloud (clouds)
Clouds float in the sky. They are usually white or grey. Clouds are made of tiny drops of water which sometimes fall as rain.

22

Aa Bb Cc Dd Ee Ff Gg Hh Ii Jj Kk Ll Mm

clown (clowns)
A clown works in a circus and wears funny clothes. Clowns paint their faces and make you laugh by doing silly things.

clue (clues)
A clue helps you to find the answer to a puzzle.

coal
Coal is hard black rock that is dug out from under the ground. It is burned to give heat.
The coal glowed red on the open fire as I warmed my hands.

coat (coats)
You wear a coat over the top of your other clothes to keep warm when you go out.

cobweb (cobwebs)
A cobweb is a fine sticky net that a spider builds for catching insects.
The fly struggled to get free from the cobweb, but it could not escape.

cocoa
Cocoa is a brown powder that is used to make a hot chocolate drink. It is also used in cooking.

coffee
Coffee is a hot drink that is made from coffee beans.

coin (coins)
A coin is a piece of metal money.

cold[1] (colds)
A cold is an illness that makes you sneeze and your nose run.

cold[2] (colder, coldest)
When the weather is cold, the temperature is low outside.

collar (collars)
1. The collar of a shirt or other piece of clothing is the part which fits around the neck.
2. A collar is a band that you put around a dog's neck.

colour[1] (colours)
There are many different colours: red, green, yellow and blue are four of them.

colour[2] (colours, colouring, coloured)
If you colour something, you use crayons or paints on it.

23

Nn Oo Pp Qq Rr Ss Tt Uu Vv Ww Xx Yy Zz

comic (comics)
A comic is a paper that has stories told in pictures.

computer
(computers)
A computer is a machine that keeps information. Computers can make other machines work and they can work things out for you.

control (controls, controlling, controlled)
If you control something, you are in charge of it and make it do what you want.
She controlled the model boat perfectly.

cook (cooks, cooking, cooked)
When you cook food, you get it ready to eat by heating it.

cooker (cookers)
A cooker is for heating food. It has a hob on top for boiling and frying and an oven underneath to bake or roast food.

cool (cooler, coolest)
If something is cool, it is nearly cold.

copper
Copper is a shiny reddish metal used for making things like water pipes.

copy
(copies, copying, copied)
1. When you copy something, you do another one exactly the same as the first.
She copied Van Gogh's 'Sunflowers' so well that I could not tell the difference.
2. If you copy something that someone does, you do the same thing as they do.
He copied Georgie's hairstyle, but it did not suit him so well!

corner
(corners)
A corner is the place where two edges, two sides or two streets meet.

cost (costs, costing, cost)
If something costs a certain amount of money, that is what you have to pay to buy it.
How much did that game cost?

cottage (cottages)
A cottage is a small house, usually in the country.

24

Aa Bb Cc Dd Ee Ff Gg Hh Ii Jj Kk Ll Mm

cotton
1. Cotton is a thread used for sewing.
2. Cotton is a light material used for making clothes.

cough (coughs, coughing, coughed)
When you cough, you make a short loud sound from your throat.
My food went the wrong way when I swallowed and it made me cough.

count
(counts, counting, counted)
1. When you count, you say numbers in order.
2. If you count things, you add them up to see how many there are.
I counted at least 42 sheep and lambs in the field outside my room.

counter (counters)
1. A counter is a small round piece of plastic used for playing some games.
2. The counter in a shop is a long table where you are served.

country (countries)
1. A country is a place which has its own people and laws. Sweden, Japan and North America are all countries.
2. The country is a place away from towns where there are fields, woods and rivers.

cousin (cousins)
Your cousin is the child of your aunt or uncle.

cover[1] (covers)
A cover is on the outside of something. Blankets or duvets are covers for a bed. Books have covers, too.

cover[2] (covers, covering, covered)
If you cover something, you put something over it to protect it or to hide it.

cow (cows)
A cow is a large farm animal that gives milk.

crack (cracks)
A crack is a thin opening on the surface of something where it has been partly broken.
There is a crack in this cup.

cracker (crackers)
1. A cracker is a thin biscuit often eaten with cheese.
2. A cracker is a tube made of decorated card. It has a small present inside it and it bangs when two people pull it apart.
There was a ring inside my Christmas cracker.

25

Nn Oo Pp Qq Rr Ss Tt Uu Vv Ww Xx Yy Zz

crane (cranes)
A crane is a machine that lifts and moves very heavy things.

crash (crashes)
1. A crash is a sudden, loud, breaking sound.
2. A crash is a road accident.

crawl (crawls, crawling, crawled)
If you crawl, you move along on your hands and knees.

crayon (crayons)
A crayon is a coloured pencil.

cream
Cream is the thick layer on top of milk.

creature (creatures)
A creature is any animal.
There are hundreds of tiny creatures in this woodland bank.

creep (creeps, creeping, crept)
1. If you creep, you move slowly and quietly so that no one will hear you.
2. An animal that creeps moves close to the ground.

crew (crews)
The crew of a boat or an aeroplane is the group of people who work together on it.
There were six men and two women in the crew.

cricket
Cricket is a game played by two teams of eleven people. It is played on a field using a ball, two bats and two wickets.

cried See **cry**

cries See **cry**

crisp[1] (crisps)
A crisp is a thin piece of potato which has been deep fried.

crisp[2] (crisper, crispest)
1. If something like a biscuit is crisp, it is dry and easy to break.
2. If an apple is crisp, it is crunchy and fresh.

26

Aa Bb Cc Dd Ee Ff Gg Hh Ii Jj Kk Ll Mm

crocodile (crocodiles)
A crocodile is a large reptile with a long body that lives in the rivers of some hot countries, such as Australia and India.

crop (crops)
Crops are plants that are grown on farms for food.
The farmer had a very good crop of wheat and barley after a warm summer.

cross[1]
(crosses)
A cross is a sign showing two lines crossing each other.

cross[2] (crosses, crossing, crossed)
If you cross a road or a river, you go from one side to the other.

cross[3] (crosser, crossest)
If you feel cross, you feel annoyed about something.
John was cross because he had forgotten his picnic lunch.

crowd (crowds)
A crowd is a large number of people gathered together in one place.
The huge crowd pushed forward to try to see the Queen.

cry (cries, crying, cried)
If you cry, you are sad and tears fall from your eyes.

cup (cups)
A cup is a small container with a handle that you use for drinking liquids.

curl[1] (curls)
A curl is a piece of hair twisted into a ring.

curl[2] (curls, curling, curled)
If a person or animal curls up, they make themselves into a little ball.

curtain (curtains)
A curtain is a piece of cloth that you pull across a window to cover it.

cut (cuts, cutting, cut)
If you cut something, you use something sharp like a knife or a pair of scissors to split it.

27

Nn Oo Pp Qq Rr Ss Tt Uu Vv Ww Xx Yy Zz

D

daily
If you do something daily, you do it each day.
My brother has a daily paper round.

dance
(dances, dancing, danced) When you dance, you move about in time to music.

28

danger
Danger is something that might hurt or harm you.

dangerous
Something dangerous can kill or hurt you badly.
It is dangerous to play with matches.

dark (darker, darkest)
If it is dark, there is no light.
It was so dark on the country road that she could not see her way.

date (dates)
1. The date is the day, month and year when something happens.
2. A date is a dried fruit which is sweet and sticky. Dates grow on palm trees.

dawn
Dawn is the first light of the day when the sun rises.
I woke up at dawn with the sunlight streaming through the window.

day (days)
1. A day is 24 hours long. A new day starts at midnight and finishes the following midnight.
2. Day is the time when it is light. It begins when the sun comes up and ends when the sun goes down.

daydream
(daydreams) When you have a daydream, you think about things that you would like to happen.

dead
Something that is dead is not alive.

deaf (deafer, deafest)
Someone who is deaf cannot hear.

December
December is the twelfth and last month of the year. It has 31 days.

Aa Bb Cc Dd Ee Ff Gg Hh Ii Jj Kk Ll Mm

decide (decides, deciding, decided)
If you decide something, you make up your mind about it.
I decided to go to the swimming pool with the others after all.

decorate (decorates, decorating, decorated)
When you decorate something, you add things to it to make it look prettier.
He decorated the living room before his grandmother moved in.

deep (deeper, deepest)
If something is deep, it goes a long way down to the bottom.
The well was so deep that they hardly heard the pebbles fall.

deer
A deer is a wild animal that can run very fast. Many deer live in groups called herds. Male deer have big horns like branches called antlers.

defend (defends, defending, defended)
When you defend something, you keep it safe from being attacked.
The soldiers defended the bridge until more help arrived.

delicious
Something delicious tastes or smells very good.
We each had a delicious ice cream at the end of the meal.

delighted
If you are delighted about something, you are very pleased about it.
Aaron was delighted to be invited to Vicki's party.

deliver (delivers, delivering, delivered)
If you deliver something, you take it to a place.
The milkman delivered four pints of milk to our house yesterday.

29

dentist (dentists)
A dentist is someone whose job it is to look after people's teeth.

describe (describes, describing, described)
When you describe something or someone, you explain exactly what they are like.

desert (deserts)
A desert is a dry sandy or stony place where it hardly ever rains. Not many plants grow in the desert.

diamond (diamonds)
A diamond is a clear precious stone which sparkles. Diamonds are worth a lot of money.
The princess had a diamond in her crown.

dictionary (dictionaries)
A dictionary is a book that tells you what words mean and how to spell them. The words are in alphabetical order.

30

die (dies, dying, died)
When someone or something dies, they stop living.
Eleanor's plants died because they hadn't been watered.

different
People or things that are different are not the same.
My hair is a different colour to yours: mine is white and yours is brown.

difficult
Something that is difficult is not easy to do.
It is difficult to do big sums in your head.

dig (digs, digging, dug)
When an animal or a person digs, they move soil away to make a hole in the ground.

dinner (dinners)
Dinner is the main meal of the day.
We had burgers, salad and chips for dinner.

dinosaur (dinosaurs)
A dinosaur is a large animal that lived on earth millions of years ago.

direction (directions)
The direction is the way you go to get somewhere.
We were driving in the wrong direction, so we had to turn around.

dirt
Dirt is dust or mud.

dirty (dirtier, dirtiest)
Something that is dirty is not clean.
Mum was furious because Dad left dirty footprints on the floor.

disappear (disappears, disappearing, disappeared)
If something or someone disappears, you cannot see them anymore.

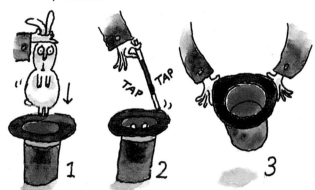

1 2 3

disappointed
If you are disappointed about something, you feel sad that what you hoped for has not happened.

disaster (disasters)
A disaster is something terrible that happens suddenly.
The earthquake was a disaster for the whole region.

discover (discovers, discovering, discovered)
If you discover something, you find out something that you did not know before.
I discovered that I had a hole in my sock when I put it on this morning.

discuss (discusses, discussing, discussed)
When you discuss something with another person, you talk and listen to each other's ideas.

dish (dishes)
A dish is a shallow bowl for food.

dishwasher (dishwashers)
A dishwasher is a machine that washes plates, pots, dishes, knives, forks, spoons and glasses.

distance (distances)
The distance between two places is how far they are from each other.

disturb (disturbs, disturbing, disturbed)
When you disturb someone, you make a noise or speak to them when they are in the middle of doing something else.
I was trying to sleep but my brother disturbed me when he turned on the radio.

dive (dives, diving, dived)
If you dive into water, you jump in head first.

divide (divides, dividing, divided)
When you divide something, you share it out into smaller parts.
I divided the chocolate bar between my three friends.

doctor (doctors)
A doctor's job is to help people to get better when they are ill.

31

Nn Oo Pp Qq Rr Ss Tt Uu Vv Ww Xx Yy Zz

dog (dogs)
A dog is an animal that people keep as pets or to do work.

doll (dolls)
A doll is a toy that looks like a baby or a small person.

donkey (donkeys)
A donkey is an animal like a horse with long ears.

door (doors)
A door is used to open and close the entrance to a building, a room, a cupboard or a car.

dragon
(dragons)
A dragon is a monster in stories. Dragons have large claws and wings and they breathe fire.

drain (drains)
A drain is a pipe for taking away waste water.

drank See **drink**

draw
(draws, drawing, drew, drawn)
When you draw, you make a picture with pencils or crayons.

dream (dreams, dreaming, dreamed, dreamt)
When you dream, you hear sounds and see pictures while you are asleep.

dress[1] (dresses)
A dress is a piece of clothing that is like a skirt and top joined together. Girls and women wear dresses.

dress[2] (dresses, dressing, dressed)
When you dress, you put your clothes on.

drew See **draw**

drift (drifts, drifting, drifted)
If something or someone drifts, they are carried along gently by water or air.
The feather drifted through the air.

drink (drinks, drinking, drank, drunk)
If you drink, you swallow something liquid like water.

Aa Bb Cc Dd Ee Ff Gg Hh Ii Jj Kk Ll Mm

drip (drips, dripping, dripped)
If something drips, drops of liquid fall from it.
Cold water dripped from the bathroom tap.

drive (drives, driving, drove, driven)
If you drive a machine such as a car, you make it move along wherever you want it to go.

drop (drops, dropping, dropped)
If you drop something, you let it fall to the ground.
The plate broke when he dropped it.

drove See **drive**

drown (drowns, drowning, drowned)
If a person or an animal drowns, they die because they cannot breathe under water.

drum (drums)
A drum is a musical instrument that you bang with your hands or with sticks.

drunk See **drink**

dry (drier, driest)
Something that is dry is not wet.

duck (ducks)
A duck is a bird that can swim and fly. It has a wide flat beak and lives near water.

dug See **dig**

dungeon (dungeons)
A dungeon is an underground prison in a castle.

dusk
Dusk is the time of day when the sun sets and it begins to get dark.
As dusk fell, the temperature dropped and we began to feel cold.

dust
Dust is dry dirt like powder.

duvet (duvets)
A duvet is a cover with a soft light filling that you use on a bed instead of blankets.

dying See **die**

33

Nn Oo Pp Qq Rr Ss Tt Uu Vv Ww Xx Yy Zz

E e

eagle (eagles)
An eagle is a large bird that hunts small animals.

ear (ears)
Your ears are the part of your body that you use for hearing and for balance.

early (earlier, earliest)
If you are early, you get to a place before you expected to.

earn (earns, earning, earned, earnt)
When you earn money, you do a job and get paid for it.

earth
1. Earth is the ground where things grow. It is another name for soil.
2. The planet we live on is called Earth.

earthquake (earthquakes)
An earthquake is a movement under the ground. Sometimes the shaking is so violent that buildings fall down.

east
East is one of the points of the compass. The sun rises in the east.

easy (easier, easiest)
Things that are easy are not difficult.

eat (eats, eating, ate, eaten)
If you eat, you take food into your body through your mouth.

echo (echoes)
An echo is a sound you have made that bounces back to you so that you can hear it again.
When he called 'Hello!', he could hear the echo of his voice from the valley.

edge (edges)
The edge of something is the top, bottom or side of it.

effect (effects)
The effect of something is the thing that happens as a result of something else.

effort (efforts)
Effort is how much you try when you are doing something.
She made a huge effort to do her sums.

34

Aa Bb Cc Dd Ee Ff Gg Hh Ii Jj Kk Ll Mm

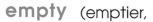

egg (eggs)
An egg is an oval or round object laid by birds, snakes, fish or insects. We can eat the eggs that hens lay.

eight
Eight is the number 8.

elastic
Something that is elastic can be pulled and stretched until you let go, and then it goes back into its own shape.

elbow (elbows)
Your elbow is the part of your body where your arm bends.
Mary bumped her elbow on the bench and it hurt!

electricity
Electricity is the power that makes many things work, such as televisions, lights, fires and cookers.

elephant (elephants)
An elephant is the biggest animal that lives on land.

It has tusks and a long nose called a trunk.

empty (emptier, emptiest)
When something is empty, it has nothing in it.

end (ends)
The end is the last part of something.

enemy (enemies)
Your enemy is someone who wants to harm you.

energetic
If you are energetic, you can keep on doing things without becoming tired.
Robert is very energetic: he runs the marathon every year.

energy (energies)
Energy is the strength to do things.

engine (engines)
An engine is a machine that makes its own power and is used to make things move or work.

35

Nn Oo Pp Qq Rr Ss Tt Uu Vv Ww Xx Yy Zz

engineer (engineers)
An engineer is someone who plans how roads, bridges or machines will be built.

enjoy (enjoys, enjoying, enjoyed)
If you enjoy doing something, you like doing it.
Felix enjoys playing on the beach.

enormous
If something is enormous, it is very very large.

enough
If you have had enough of something, you do not want any more of it.

enter (enters, entering, entered)
When you enter a place, you go in.

entrance (entrances)
The entrance to a place is the way in.
The entrance was blocked so they had to wait before they could go in.

envelope (envelopes)
An envelope is the paper cover that you put a letter in before posting it.

To
Timothy Reeves,
15 Main Street,
Beresford
BS4 7AW

environment (environments)
Your environment is everything around you.
Sophie grew up in an environment of busy streets and noisy traffic.

equal
If two or more things are equal, they are the same.

equipment
Equipment is all the things you need to do something.
They put all their camping equipment in the back of the car but they forgot the sleeping bags.

escape (escapes, escaping, escaped)
If you escape, you get away from whoever or whatever is keeping you in one place.

estate (estates)
An estate is an area of land with lots of houses on it.
My best friend lives on a housing estate.

Aa Bb Cc Dd Ee Ff Gg Hh Ii Jj Kk Ll Mm

even
1. Something that is even is smooth.
The road had an even surface, so we had a smooth ride.
2. If a number is even, it can be divided by two with nothing left over.

evening
(evenings)
The evening is the time at the end of the day before night begins.

evil
Evil means very wicked. Evil people do things to harm others.

excited
If you are excited, you are very happy and interested in something.
Jeremy was very excited at the thought of going abroad.

excuse (excuses)
If you make an excuse, you try to explain why you did something wrong.
What is your excuse for being late?

exhausted
If you are exhausted, you are very tired indeed.

exit (exits)
An exit is a way out of a place.

expect (expects, expecting, expected)
If you expect something to happen, you are sure that it will.
Sam expected to get £20 from his father for his birthday.

explain (explains, explaining, explained)
When you explain something to someone, you tell them all about it as clearly as you can.

explode (explodes, exploding, exploded)
If something explodes, it bursts with a very loud bang.

37

explore (explores, exploring, explored)
When you explore, you look around a place for the first time.

extinct
When an animal is extinct, there are no more of its kind left in the world.

extra
Something extra is more than the usual amount.

eye (eyes)
The eyes of a person or an animal are the parts they see with.

face (faces)
Your face is the front of your head where your eyes, nose and mouth are.

fact (facts)
A fact is something that is true and is not made up.
It is a fact that you can cook food very quickly in a microwave oven.

38 **factory** (factories)
A factory is a building where goods are made by machines.

fail (fails, failing, failed)
If you fail to do something, you do not manage to do it.
Our team failed to score a goal and so we lost the game.

fair¹ (fairs)
A fair is a place where people have fun on roundabouts, stalls and rides.

fair² (fairer, fairest)
1. If you are fair, your hair is light in colour.
2. If you are fair when playing a game, you do not cheat.

fairy (fairies)
A fairy is a tiny imaginary creature with magic powers. You can read about fairies in story books.

fall (falls, falling, fell, fallen)
If something falls, it drops down to the ground suddenly.
The milk bottle fell down the steps.

family (families)
1. A family is parents and their children.
2. A family is a set of relations such as grandparents, uncles, aunts and cousins.

famous
If someone is famous, they are very well-known.

far (farther, farthest)
Far is a long way away.

London 126 miles

farm (farms)
A farm is a large area of land where a farmer keeps animals or grows crops for food.

Aa Bb Cc Dd Ee Ff Gg Hh Ii Jj Kk Ll Mm

fast (faster, fastest)
If something is fast, it is quick.
My sister can run faster than I can.

fasten (fastens, fastening, fastened)
When you fasten something, you close it or do it up.

fat[1] (fats)
1. Fat is the greasy part of meat.
She ate all the meat except for the fat.
2. Fat is used for cooking. Butter and oil are both fats.

fat[2] (fatter, fattest)
If someone is fat, they have too much flesh on their body.

father (fathers)
A father is a man who has his own child or children.

fault (faults)
1. If something is your fault, you made it happen.
It was Trevor's fault that they missed the bus: he forgot to set his alarm clock.
2. A fault spoils something that is perfect in every other way.
There was a fault in the material so she did not buy it.

favourite
Your favourite thing is the one you like the best.

fear (fears)
Fear is a feeling that you get when you are frightened that something unpleasant will happen.

feast (feasts)
A feast is a large special meal with lots of delicious things to eat and drink.

feather (feathers)
A feather is one of the many very light pieces that make up the covering of a bird's body.

February
February is the second month of the year. It usually has 28 days, but once every four years it has 29 days.

39

feed (feeds, feeding, fed)
When you feed someone, you give them food.

feel (feels, feeling, felt)
1. If you feel sad, happy or ill, that is the way you are at the time.
2. If you feel something, you touch it to see what it is like.

Nn Oo Pp Qq Rr Ss Tt Uu Vv Ww Xx Yy Zz

feet See **foot**

fell See **fall**

felt See **feel**

female (females)
Any person or animal that is female can become a mother.

fence (fences)
A fence is something put round a piece of land to keep animals or people in or out.

ferry (ferries)
A ferry takes people and cars across a stretch of water.

40

festival (festivals)
A festival is a celebration of something, where people dance and play music.

fetch (fetches, fetching, fetched)
When you fetch something, you go and get it.
My dog fetched the frisbee from the bottom of the garden.

fete (fetes)
A fete is a kind of open air party with competitions and stalls for selling cakes, toys and many other things. It is usually held to raise money for charity.

fever (fevers)
A fever is an illness that makes you feel very hot, weak and thirsty.

few (fewer, fewest)
A few means not many.
By the time I got home from the sweet shop, I only had a few chocolates left!

field (fields)
A field is an open piece of land with a fence or a hedge around it.

fifty
Fifty is the number 50.

fight (fights, fighting, fought)
When people or animals fight, they try to hurt each other.
I could hear the cats fighting again last night.

fill (fills, filling, filled)
If you fill something, you put so much in it that there is no room for any more.

film (films)
1. A film is moving pictures shown on screen which tell a story.
2. A film is a roll of plastic you put in a camera to take photographs.
I forgot to put the film in my camera so I don't have any holiday photos.

Aa Bb Cc Dd Ee Ff Gg Hh Ii Jj Kk Ll Mm

fin (fins)
A fin is the part of a fish that is like a small spiny or filmy wing. A fish uses its fins to swim.

find (finds, finding, found)
If you find something after you have lost it, you come across it again.

fine¹ (fines)
If you are given a fine, you have to pay a sum of money because you have done something wrong.
If you park your car on a double yellow line, you will get a fine.

fine² (finer, finest)
If something is fine, it is very good indeed.

finger (fingers)
Your finger is part of your hand. You have four fingers and a thumb on each hand.

finish (finishes, finishing, finished)
If you finish something, you get to the end of it.

fire (fires)
A fire is something that burns to keep people warm or to give light.

firework (fireworks)
A firework is a cardboard tube filled with gunpowder. When you set light to it, it explodes, sometimes with a bang, making brightly-coloured patterns in the sky.

firm (firmer, firmest)
If something is firm, it is strong and does not give way when you press it.
The bridge felt firm so I did not mind walking across it.

first
First means before anyone or anything else.
Peter came first in the sack race.

fish (fish or fishes)
A fish is a creature which lives in water. It has fins, is covered with scales and breathes through gills.

fisherman (fishermen)
A fisherman catches fish for a living or for sport.

fit¹ (fits, fitting, fitted, fit)
If something fits, it is the right size and shape.

fit² (fitter, fittest)
If you are fit, you are healthy.
He was fit because he ate good food and had plenty of exercise.

41

Nn Oo Pp Qq Rr Ss Tt Uu Vv Ww Xx Yy Zz

five
Five is the number 5.

fix (fixes, fixing, fixed)
1. If you fix something, you mend it.
2. If you fix one thing to another, you tie them both firmly together.

flame (flames)
A flame is the bright fire that leaps from something burning.

flash (flashes, flashing, flashed)
A flash is a sudden bright light that lasts for just a moment.
The lightning flashed for a second, then we heard a roar of thunder.

42

flat¹ (flats)
A flat is a group of rooms on one floor in a large building where people live.

flat² (flatter, flattest)
If something is flat, it has no bumps in it.

flavour (flavours)
The flavour of something is how it tastes.
Jo's favourite ice cream was mint flavour.

flew See **fly²**

flies See **fly²**

float (floats, floating, floated)
If something floats on liquid, it rests on the top.

flock (flocks)
A flock is a large group of birds or sheep.

flood (floods)
A flood is a huge amount of water that spreads over a large area of dry land.

floor (floors)
The floor is the flat part of a room that you walk on.

flour
Flour is a white or brown powder made from wheat. It is used to make things like bread and cakes.

flow (flows, flowing, flowed)
When water flows, it runs freely and smoothly.

flower (flowers)
A flower is the coloured part of a plant that holds the seeds.

flown See **fly²**

fly¹ (flies)
A fly is a small insect with one pair of wings.

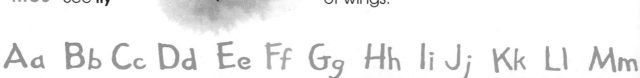

Aa Bb Cc Dd Ee Ff Gg Hh Ii Jj Kk Ll Mm

F

fly² (flies, flying, flew, flown)
If a bird, a plane or an insect flies, it travels through the air.

follow (follows, following, followed)
1. If you follow someone or something, you go after it.
My dog followed me down the road.
2. If you follow a path, you go along it.

food (food or foods)
Food is what we eat to keep alive.

foot (feet)
Your foot is the part of your body that you stand on.

football
Football is a team game where the players try to score goals by kicking a ball into a net.

foreign
People or things that are foreign come from another country.
Henry collected foreign stamps. His favourites were from Thailand.

forest (forests)
A forest is a large area of land covered with trees growing closely together.

forgave See **forgive**

forget (forgets, forgetting, forgot, forgotten)
When you forget something, you cannot remember it even though you knew it before.
I put the letter in a safe place, but then I forgot where it was.

forgive (forgives, forgiving, forgave, forgiven)
When you forgive someone, you stop being cross with them for whatever it was they did wrong.

forgot See **forget**

forgotten See **forget**

fork (forks)
A fork is a tool with prongs that you use to pick up food.

fought See **fight**

forward
If you move forward, you move towards the front.

Joel moved his chess piece forward.

found See **find**

four
Four is the number 4.

43

fox (foxes)
A fox is a red-brown wild animal with a bushy tail.

frame (frames)
A frame is the wood or metal surround of a picture, photograph, window or mirror.

free (freer, freest)
1. If you are free, there is nothing to stop you from doing anything you want to do.
2. If something is free, you do not have to pay for it.

freeze (freezes, freezing, froze, frozen)
If something freezes, it becomes hard because of the cold.
It was so cold that the water froze in the pipes.

fresh (fresher, freshest)
If something is fresh, it is new.

Friday
Friday is the day after Thursday and before Saturday.

fridge (fridges)
Fridge is short for refrigerator.

friend (friends)
A friend is someone you know well and like a lot.

frighten (frightens, frightening, frightened)
If you frighten someone, you make them afraid.
Kamal frightened Jim when he dressed up as a ghost.

frog (frogs)
A frog is a small animal with smooth skin, big eyes and long back legs. Frogs live near water and can jump a long way.

front
The front of anything is the face of it.

froze See **freeze**

frozen See **freeze**

fruit (fruit or fruits)
Fruit is the part of a tree or plant that holds the seeds. You can eat the part around the seeds or the stone.

fry (fries, frying, fried)
If you fry something, you cook it in a pan with hot fat.

44

fuel
Fuel is something that can be burned to make heat.
They gathered wood for fuel so they could make a bonfire on the beach.

full (fuller, fullest)
If something is full, there is no room for any more to fit in.

fun
If you have fun, you enjoy yourself and do things that make you happy.

funny (funnier, funniest)
Something funny makes you laugh.

fur (furs)
Fur is the soft hair that grows on animals.

furniture
Furniture is all the things you use in a house like beds, tables, chairs and cupboards.

fuss (fusses, fussing, fussed)
If you fuss, you worry too much about something that is not important.

gale (gales)
A gale is a storm with very strong winds and heavy rain.

game (games)
A game is something you play for fun. It can be with toys or with other people. Sometimes games have rules.

gap (gaps)
A gap is a small space between two things.
The dentist put a brace on Carol's teeth to make the gap join up.

garage (garages)
A garage is a place where a car is kept or repaired.

garden (gardens)
A garden is land next to someone's house where they can grow flowers, trees and vegetables.

45

gas (gases)
Gas is like air. It burns easily and gives light and heat. Gas is used for cooking.

gate (gates)
A gate is like a door in a hedge or a wall. *The gate had been left open, so all the cows got out.*

gather (gathers, gathering, gathered)
If people or animals gather, they come together in a group.

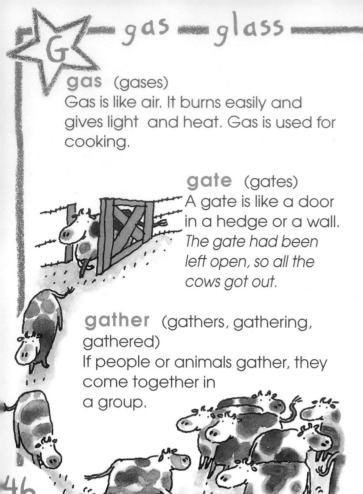

46

gave See **give**

gentle (gentler, gentlest)
Gentle is soft, quiet and kind. *You must be very gentle with little babies.*

gentleman (gentlemen)
A gentleman is a polite name for a man.

gerbil (gerbils)
A gerbil is a small furry animal with very long back legs. Gerbils like to burrow and are often kept in an aquarium filled with sand and sawdust.

ghost (ghosts)
A ghost is the spirit of a dead person that some people think they can see.

giant (giants)
A giant is a huge person in fairy stories.

gift (gifts)
A gift is a present.

giraffe (giraffes)
A giraffe is a very tall animal with a long neck.

girl (girls)
A girl is a child who will be a woman when she is older.

give (gives, giving, gave, given)
If you give someone something, you let them have it.

glass
1. Glass is something hard that you can see through and which breaks easily. *The burglar broke the glass to get into the house.*
2. (glasses) A glass is a cup made of glass.

Aa Bb Cc Dd Ee Ff Gg Hh Ii Jj Kk Ll Mm

glasses
A pair of glasses is two pieces of glass lenses joined together in a frame. People who cannot see very well wear glasses.

gloomy (gloomier, gloomiest)
1. When it is gloomy, it is dark.
2. If you feel gloomy, you feel sad.

glossary (glossaries)
A glossary is a list of words and their meanings that you find at the back of a book.
Ben didn't know what the word meant, so he looked it up in the glossary.

glove (gloves)
A glove is a covering for your hand to protect it or to keep it warm.

glue (glues)
Glue is a strong paste or liquid for sticking things together.

goal (goals)
In games such as football and basketball, a goal is the space into which players try to get the ball to score a point.

goat (goats)
A goat is an animal that is kept mainly for its milk. It has coarse hair, horns and a short tail.

gold
Gold is a precious metal.

good (better, best)
1. If a person or animal is good, it is well-behaved.
2. If music, painting or a play is good, it is enjoyable.
3. Someone who is good is caring and kind.

goose (geese)
A goose is a large bird that swims, flies and lays eggs. It is bigger than a duck and has a long beak.

gorilla (gorillas)
A gorilla is the largest of the apes. Gorillas live in African forests in family groups. They eat fruit and leaves.

grain (grains)
Grain is the seeds of some plants that are used for food.

grandfather (grandfathers)
Your grandfather is the father of your mother or your father. Some people call their grandfather grandpa or grandad.

47

Nn Oo Pp Qq Rr Ss Tt Uu Vv Ww Xx Yy Zz

grandmother (grandmothers)
Your grandmother is the mother of your mother or your father. Some people call their grandmother grandma or granny.

grape (grapes)
A grape is a small soft green or purple fruit that grows in bunches.

grass (grasses)
Grass is the thin green leaves that grow thickly in fields and on lawns and hillsides.

great (greater, greatest)
Great is something very big, grand and wonderful.
The party was a great success.

48

greedy (greedier, greediest)
Greedy people and animals eat more than they need.

green (greener, greenest)
Green is the colour of grass and trees.

grew See **grow**

grey (greyer, greyest)
Grey is the colour of the sky when it rains.

groan (groans, groaning, groaned)
If you groan, you make a low moaning sound because you are unhappy or in pain.

ground
The ground is the earth beneath your feet.

group (groups)
A group is a number of people or things which are together in one place.

grow (grows, growing, grew, grown)
If something grows, it gets bigger.

1   2   3

growl (growls, growling, growled)
When a dog growls, it makes a deep, rumbling, angry sound.
The dog growled at the stranger.

grown See **grow**

Aa Bb Cc Dd Ee Ff Gg Hh Ii Jj Kk Ll Mm

grunt (grunts, grunting, grunted)
A grunt is a low rough noise made by a pig.

guard (guards)
A guard is a person who watches over people, places or objects to keep them safe.

guess (guesses, guessing, guessed)
If you make a guess, you give an answer to a question when you do not really know the answer.

guide (guides)
A guide is a person who shows people the way to go.
The guide took us round the castle and told us all about it.

guitar (guitars)
A guitar is a musical instrument with strings. You play it with your fingers.

gun (guns)
A gun is a weapon that shoots bullets.

hair (hair or hairs)
Hair grows on the heads and bodies of people and animals. It is made up of thousands of pieces.

half (halves)
If you cut something exactly through the middle, you cut it in half. Two halves are equal.

hall (halls)
The hall in a house is the space inside the front door that leads to other rooms.
We left our umbrellas in the hall.

hammer (hammers)
A hammer is a tool with a handle and a heavy head for hitting nails into wood and other surfaces.

hamster (hamsters)
A hamster is a small furry animal that can be kept as a pet.

49

Nn Oo Pp Qq Rr Ss Tt Uu Vv Ww Xx Yy Zz

hand (hands)
Your hand is at the end of your arm.

handle[1] (handles)
Handles are put onto things such as cups, saucepans and doors to make them easier to hold, carry or open.

handle[2] (handles, handling, handled)
If you handle something, you touch, feel or hold it with your hands.
Dorothy handled the seedlings carefully as she put them into the ground.

hang (hangs, hanging, hung)
If you hang something up, you put it on a hook so it does not touch the ground.

happen (happens, happening, happened)
When something happens, it takes place.

happy (happier, happiest)
When you are happy, you feel pleased about something.
Tina was happy to hear that her grandmother had come out of hospital.

hard (harder, hardest)
1. If something is hard, it is not soft.
The ground was hard and dry after weeks without rain.
2. If something is hard to do, it is difficult.

hare (hares)
A hare is an animal like a large rabbit with long ears and long legs. Hares can move very fast.

harness (harnesses)
A harness is a set of straps that is put over a horse's head and neck so that you can control the horse while you are riding it.

hat (hats)
A hat is a covering for your head.

hatch (hatches, hatching, hatched)
When something hatches, it comes out of an egg.
A tiny alligator hatched out of its shell.

hate (hates, hating, hated)
If you hate someone, you do not like them at all.

50

Aa Bb Cc Dd Ee Ff Gg Hh Ii Jj Kk Ll Mm

hay
Hay is dry grass which is used to feed animals.

head (heads)
Your head is above your neck. It holds your brain, eyes, ears, nose and mouth.

headache (headaches)
A headache is a pain in your head.

health
Health is how your body feels. Your health depends on whether you are feeling well or ill.

healthy (healthier, healthiest)
If you are healthy, you are free from illness.
They were a very healthy family – not one of them had been to hospital.

hear (hears, hearing, heard)
When you hear things, you notice sounds through your ears.

heart (hearts)
1. Your heart is the part of your body that pumps blood around inside you.
2. A heart is also a shape that looks a bit like the heart in your body.

heaven
Heaven is the place where God is believed to live.

heavy (heavier, heaviest)
Something heavy is difficult to lift or carry.

hedge (hedges)
A hedge is a row of bushes growing closely together.

hedgehog (hedgehogs)
A hedgehog is a small brown animal which is covered in prickles.

held See **hold**

51

helicopter (helicopters)
A helicopter is a small aircraft with blades instead of wings. The blades on its roof spin round to make it hover, fly forward or go straight up. The tail blades make it balance.

help (helps, helping, helped)
If you help someone, you make things easier for them.

Nn Oo Pp Qq Rr Ss Tt Uu Vv Ww Xx Yy Zz

hen (hens)
A hen is a chicken that lays eggs.

herd (herds)
A herd is a group of animals, such as sheep or cows, that are kept together.

hero (heroes)
A hero is a boy or a man who has done something very brave. A girl or woman who has done something very brave is a heroine.

hide (hides, hiding, hid, hidden)
If you hide from somebody, you put yourself somewhere where they can't find you.

52

high (higher, highest)
Something that is high goes up a long way.
The kite flew high in the sky.

hill (hills)
A hill is ground which is higher than the ground around it.

hippopotamus
(hippopotamuses hippopotami)
A hippopotamus is a large heavy African animal that spends a great deal of time in rivers and lakes.

history
History is time in the past. When we study history, we find out about the lives and times of people who lived long ago.

hit (hits, hitting, hit)
If you hit something or someone, you strike them or knock them.

hive (hives)
A hive is a place where people keep bees. On the inside there are places for the bees to build their honeycombs.

hold (holds, holding, held)
When you hold something, you take it in your hands or arms.
Susie tried to hold on to the rope, but her hands were wet and it slipped away.

hole (holes)
A hole is an opening in something.

holiday (holidays)
A holiday is time off from school or work when people rest or have a good time.

hollow
If something is hollow, it has an empty space inside it.
A toad lived inside the hollow tree.

home (homes)
A home is a place to live.

honey
Honey is the sweet yellow liquid that bees make. People often eat honey on bread.

hoof (hooves)
A hoof is the hard part of a horse's foot. Cattle, deer and some other animals have hooves.

deer   horse   cow

hop (hops, hopping, hopped)
If you hop, you jump up and down on one foot.

hope (hopes, hoping, hoped)
If you hope for something, you wish it to be true.

horn (horns)
A horn is one of the sharp bony parts that grow out of the head of some animals. Cows, goats and deer have horns.

horrible
Horrible means dreadful, nasty or frightening.

horse (horses)
A horse is a large animal which people ride. Some horses are used for pulling carts or farm machinery.

hospital (hospitals)
A hospital is a place where people go to be cared for by doctors and nurses when they are sick or hurt.

hot (hotter, hottest)
Something hot is very warm.

hour (hours)
An hour is a length of time. It is made up of 60 minutes. A day has 24 hours in it.

house (houses)
A house is a building where people live together.

hover (hovers, hovering, hovered)
If something hovers, it floats or stays in one place in the air.
I watched the dragonfly hover over the pond.

huge
Something huge is very very big.

human (humans)
A human is a man, woman or child.

hurt (hurts, hurting, hurt)
If you hurt yourself, you feel pain.

53

Nn Oo Pp Qq Rr Ss Tt Uu Vv Ww Xx Yy Zz

ice
Ice is water that has frozen hard.
Last winter the pond was covered with ice.

ice cream
Ice cream is a frozen food made with milk, sugar and flavouring.

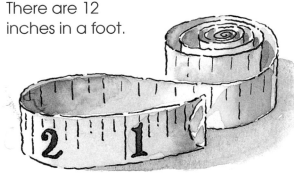

54

idea (ideas)
An idea is something that you have thought of yourself.
Amanda had a good idea – she could make jam to raise money for the donkey farm.

ill
If you are ill, you do not feel well because there is something wrong with you.

imagine (imagines, imagining, imagined)
When you imagine something, you picture how it would be in your mind.

immediately
If you do something immediately, you do it at once.

important
Something or someone important is special, clever or powerful.

impossible
Something that is impossible cannot be done.
It was impossible to untie the knot, so they cut the rope instead.

inch (inches)
An inch is a measure of length. There are 12 inches in a foot.

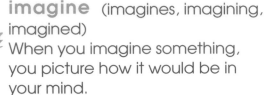

index (indexes)
An index is a list in alphabetical order at the back of a book. It tells you where to find things in the book.

information
Information is a collection of facts that tell you about something.

Aa Bb Cc Dd Ee Ff Gg Hh Ii Jj Kk Ll Mm

initial (initials)
An initial is the first letter of a word or a name.

ink (inks)
Ink is a coloured liquid used with a pen for writing.

insect (insects)
An insect is a very small animal with six legs.

instruction (instructions)
If you give someone an instruction, you tell them exactly what to do.

instrument (instruments)
1. An instrument is something you use to help you do a job.
2. A musical instrument is something that you use to make sounds.

interesting
Interesting things make you want to find out more about them.
The story was so interesting that Ben read all night to finish the book.

interrupt (interrupts, interrupting, interrupted)
If you interrupt somebody, you stop them saying or doing something for a short time.

introduction (introductions)
The introduction at the beginning of a book tells you about what is in the book.

invisible
If something or somebody is invisible, you cannot see them.

invite (invites, inviting, invited)
When you invite someone, you ask them if they would like to do something.
Cathy invited six friends to her party.

55

iron
1. Iron is a strong heavy metal.
2. (irons) An iron is a flat piece of metal with a handle that you can heat and use to make your clothes smooth and flat.

island (islands)
An island is a piece of land with water all around it.

Nn Oo Pp Qq Rr Ss Tt Uu Vv Ww Xx Yy Zz

jet (jets)
A jet is a very fast plane.

jewel (jewels)
A jewel is a precious stone.
The queen's crown was covered with jewels.

jewellery
Jewellery is the name given to things that people wear to decorate themselves, such as necklaces, earrings and bracelets.

jam¹ (jams)
Jam is made from fruit boiled with sugar until it is thick and soft.

jam² (jams, jamming, jammed)
If something jams, it gets stuck.

56

January
January is the first month of the year. It has 31 days.

jar (jars)
A jar is a glass container.

jealous
If you feel jealous of somebody, you are cross because they have something you would like to have.
Nick was jealous of Jamie because he had a new football.

jigsaw (jigsaws)
A jigsaw is a puzzle made of odd-shaped pieces that make a picture when you put them together.
When the pieces of the jigsaw were put together, they made a picture of a cow.

jelly (jellies)
A jelly is a fruit-flavoured wobbly food that you often eat at parties.

job (jobs)
A job is work that someone does for money.

Aa Bb Cc Dd Ee Ff Gg Hh Ii Jj Kk Ll Mm

join (joins, joining, joined)
When you join something, you put two or more parts together to make one thing.

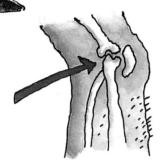

joint (joints)
A joint in your body is a place where two parts of bone fit together. Your knees, ankles and elbows are all joints.

joke (jokes)
A joke is something a person says or does to make you laugh.

journey (journeys)
If you go on a journey, you travel from one place to another.

jug (jugs)
A jug is a container with a handle which is used for pouring milk and other liquids.

juice (juice or juices)
Juice is the liquid that comes out of fruit when you squeeze it.

July
July is the seventh month of the year. It has 31 days.

jump (jumps, jumping, jumped)
When you jump, you move up in the air with both feet off the ground.

jumper
A jumper is a piece of clothing, usually made of wool, that you wear to keep warm.

June
June is the sixth month of the year. It has 30 days.

jungle (jungles)
A jungle is a forest in a hot country. The trees in a jungle are very tall and grow closely together.

57

Nn Oo Pp Qq Rr Ss Tt Uu Vv Ww Xx Yy Zz

K

kangaroo (kangaroos)
A kangaroo is an animal that lives in Australia. It has a pouch where its baby spends the first few months of its life.

keep (keeps, keeping, kept)
If you keep something, you have it for yourself.
James bought the model for his friend, but liked it so much he decided to keep it for himself.

58

kennel (kennels)
A kennel is a house for a dog.

kept See **keep**

kettle (kettles)
A kettle is a metal or plastic container with a lid that you use for boiling water.

key (keys)
A key is a small piece of metal, specially shaped so that it will open a lock.
They couldn't open the box because the key had been lost long ago.

kick (kicks, kicking, kicked)
If you kick something like a ball, you hit it hard with your foot.

kill (kills, killing, killed)
To kill is to cause the death of an animal or a person.

kilometre (kilometres)
A kilometre is a measure of length. One kilometre is 1,000 metres.

kind[1] (kinds)
The kind of something is the type or sort it is.
There were two kinds of sweet to choose from: the chocolate drops or the barley sugars.

kind[2] (kinder, kindest)
A kind person is caring and loving to other people.

Aa Bb Cc Dd Ee Ff Gg Hh Ii Jj Kk Ll Mm

king (kings)
A king is the man who rules a country.

kiss (kisses, kissing, kissed)
If you kiss someone, you touch them with your lips.

kitchen (kitchens)
A kitchen is the room in a house where food is cooked and the washing-up is done.

kite (kites)
A kite is a toy made of paper or cloth over a very light frame. You can fly it in the air on a windy day.

kitten (kittens)
A kitten is a baby cat.

knee (knees)
Your knee is the joint in your leg. It is the place where your leg bends.

kneel (kneels, kneeling, knelt)
When you kneel, you get down on your knees.

knew See **know**

knife (knives)
A knife is a thin sharp piece of metal with a handle that you use for cutting things such as meat.

knit (knits, knitting, knitted)
When you knit, you use wool and a pair of needles to make clothes like jumpers.

knock (knocks, knocking, knocked)
If you knock something, you hit it hard or bump into it.

knot (knots)
A knot is the place where two pieces of string, ribbon or wool are tied together.

know (knows, knowing, knew, known)
If you know something, you are completely sure about it.
I know that I am right because I looked up the answer in a book.

Nn Oo Pp Qq Rr Ss Tt Uu Vv Ww Xx Yy Zz

L

label (labels)
A label is paper or card that you write on and attach to things like luggage, jars and boxes so that you know what is inside.

lace (laces)
1. A lace is a piece of thick string you use to fasten your shoe.
2. Lace is a fine material made with a pattern of holes in it.

60

ladder (ladders)
A ladder is made of two long poles with short bars between them so that you can climb up and down.

lady
(ladies)
Lady is a polite name for a woman.

ladybird (ladybirds)
A ladybird is a small flying beetle that is usually red with black spots.

laid See **lay**[1]

lain See **lie**[1]

lake (lakes)
A lake is an area of fresh water with land all around it.

lamb (lambs)
A lamb is a baby sheep.

lamp (lamps)
A lamp is a light that you can move from place to place.

land[1]
Land is dry ground.

land[2] (lands, landing, landed)
If a boat or an aeroplane lands, it arrives.

lane (lanes)
A lane is a narrow road usually in the country.

language (languages)
1. Language is human speech or writing.
2. A language is the particular way people speak in different countries.
Jo is learning two languages at school: French and Spanish.

lap[1] (laps)
1. Your lap is the top part of your legs when you are sitting down.
2. A lap is the distance once around a race track.

Aa Bb Cc Dd Ee Ff Gg Hh Ii Jj Kk Ll Mm

lap[2] (laps, lapping, lapped)
When an animal laps, it drinks using its tongue.
As the cat lapped the milk, it spilled onto the floor.

large (larger, largest)
Something large is big.

late (later, latest)
If you are late at a place, you arrive after the time that you planned to be there.

laugh (laughs, laughing, laughed)
When you laugh, you make the sound that people make when they are happy or think something is funny.

law (laws)
A law is a rule that everyone in the land must keep.
He broke the law and was sent to prison.

lawn (lawns)
A lawn is a grassy area in a garden which is kept cut short.

lay[1] (lays, laying, laid)
1. When you lay the table, you get it ready for a meal.
2. When a bird lays an egg, the egg comes out of its body.
3. When you lay something down, you put it down carefully.

lay[2] See **lie**[1]

layer (layers)
A layer is a flat area that lies over or under another surface.
Mum made a cake with cream and jam between layers of sponge.

lazy (lazier, laziest)
Someone who is lazy does not want to work or do anything hard.
Jack was so lazy that he didn't even bother to get up in the morning.

lead[1] (leads) (rhymes with feed)
A lead is a long piece of leather, chain or strong fabric that you fix to a dog's collar.

lead[2] (rhymes with fed)
Lead is a very heavy soft grey metal.

61

Nn Oo Pp Qq Rr Ss Tt Uu Vv Ww Xx Yy Zz

lead — letter

L

lead³ (leads, leading, led)
(rhymes with feed)
If you lead someone to a place, you take them there to show them the way.

leader (leaders)
The leader is the person who is in front or who is in charge.

leaf
(leaves)
A leaf is one of the thin flat parts of a plant. Leaves are usually green.

leap (leaps, leaping, leapt)
If you leap, you jump a long way.

62

learn (learns, learning, learnt)
When you learn about something, you find out about it.

leather
Leather is the skin of animals when it is used to make things like shoes, handbags and jackets.

leave (leaves, leaving, left)
1. If you leave something behind, you do not take it with you.
2. If you leave a place, you go away from it.

led See **lead**³

left¹ See **leave**

left²
Your left is the opposite to your right. *Bobby lost his left glove.*

leg (legs)
Your legs are the two long parts of your body that you use for walking.

lemon (lemons)
A lemon is a sharp-tasting yellow fruit.

lemonade
Lemonade is a drink made from the juice of lemons. It is usually fizzy and sweet.

length (lengths)
The length of something is how long it is.

lens (lenses)
A lens is a curved piece of glass or plastic used in telescopes, cameras and eye glasses. Lenses make things look larger or smaller.

lesson (lessons)
A lesson is the time when your teacher is teaching you.

letter (letters)
A letter is a message that someone sends to you through the post or that they deliver by hand.

Aa Bb Cc Dd Ee Ff Gg Hh Ii Jj Kk Ll Mm

level
If something is level, it is flat.

lever (levers)
A lever is a bar that is pushed down at one end so that it lifts something at the other end.

library (libraries)
A library is a place where there is a large collection of books. You can borrow books from a public library.

lick (licks, licking, licked)
If you lick something, you move your tongue across it.

lid (lids)
A lid is the top of a box or container which can be taken off to get inside.

lie[1] (lies, lying, lay, lain)
If you lie somewhere, you rest your body flat on something.

lie[2] (lies, lying, lied)
If you lie to someone, you tell them something that is not true.
I knew he was lying because he went bright red.

life (lives)
Life is being alive. Humans, plants and animals all have life.

lifeboat (lifeboats)
A lifeboat is a boat that rescues people who are in danger at sea.

lift (lifts, lifting, lifted)
If you lift something, you move it up to a higher place.

light[1]
Light is the brightness that lets you see. Light comes from the sun, the moon, candles, fire and lamps.

light[2] (lights, lighting, lit)
When you light something, you set fire to it.
The weather was cold so they lit a fire.

light[3] (lighter, lightest)
If something is light, it is not heavy.

lighthouse (lighthouses)
A lighthouse is a tower built by the sea. It has a strong flashing light at the top to guide ships or to warn them of danger.

63

Nn Oo Pp Qq Rr Ss Tt Uu Vv Ww Xx Yy Zz

lightning
Lightning is a bright and sudden flash of light in the sky which happens during a thunderstorm.

like[1] (likes, liking, liked)
If you like something or someone, you are fond of them.

like[2]
If one thing is like another, it is nearly the same.

likely
If something is likely to happen, it probably will happen.

line (lines)
A line is a thin mark.

lion (lions)
A lion is a large animal that belongs to the cat family. Lions live in Africa and southern Asia. A female lion is called a lioness.

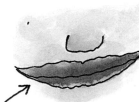

lip (lips)
Your lips are the soft red parts at the edge of your mouth.

liquid (liquids)
A liquid is anything that is wet and flows like water.
Fred broke the glass and the liquid spilled all over the floor.

list (lists)
A list is a set of things that you write down one after the other.

listen (listens, listening, listened)
When you listen, you hear what someone else is saying and you pay attention to it.

lit See **light**[2]

litter
Litter is rubbish such as waste paper and empty bottles left lying around.
People had left litter all over the park.

little
If something is little, it is very small.

live (lives, living, lived)
If something lives, it is alive.

lively
Lively means full of life and energy.

lizard (lizards)
A lizard is a small creature with four short legs and a long tail. Lizards are reptiles and have rough dry skins.

64

load (loads, loading, loaded)
If someone loads a vehicle, they put things in it to take them somewhere else.
They loaded the car ready to go away on holiday.

local
If something is local, it belongs to that area.
It only takes five minutes to walk to the local butcher's.

lock (locks)
A lock is a strong fastening for a door or a gate that can only be opened by a key.

lolly (lollies)
A lolly is a sweet or an ice on a stick.

lonely
If you are lonely, you have no friends and feel unhappy.
The old lady was lonely until Matilda the cat came to live with her.

long (longer, longest)
1. If something takes a long time, it takes a great deal of time.
2. If a road is long, it is a great distance from one end to the other.

look (looks, looking, looked)
If you look at something, you use your eyes to see what is there.

loop (loops)
A loop is a ring of something like wire, thread or ribbon.

loose (looser, loosest)
If something is loose, it is not tight.
The knot was too loose, so the balloon blew away.

lorry (lorries)
A lorry is a large truck that carries heavy loads for long distances.

lose (loses, losing, lost)
1. If you lose something, you are not able to find it.
2. If you lose a game, you do not win.

lost
If someone is lost, they cannot find their way.

loud (louder, loudest)
Something loud makes a lot of noise and is easy to hear.
The music was so loud that we could hear it next door.

love (loves, loving, loved)
If you love someone or something, you like them very much.

lovely (lovelier, loveliest)
Something lovely is beautiful to look at or listen to.

65

low (lower, lowest)
Something that is low is close to the ground.

lower (lowers, lowering, lowered)
If you lower something, you slowly move it closer to the ground.
They had to lower the man gently from the ambulance to the ground.

lowing
Lowing is the deep long sound that cattle make.

Daily News
Lucky cat wins lottery

luck
Luck is something good that happens without any reason to explain it.

lucky (luckier, luckiest)
Someone who is lucky has good luck.

lump (lumps)
A lump is a piece of something solid.

lunch (lunches)
Lunch is the meal that you have in the middle of the day.

lunchtime
Lunchtime is the time between morning and afternoon when you have a break to eat a meal.

lying See **lie**

machine (machines)
A machine is something with several parts that work together to do a job. Machines usually work by electricity or have an engine. Cars, computers and cookers are all machines.

machinery
Machinery means a collection of machines.

made See **make**

magazine (magazines)
A magazine is a thin book that comes out every week or every month. It can have stories, pictures, recipes and information in it.

magic
In fairy tales magic is a special power that can make impossible things happen.
The witch used her magic to change the prince into a frog.

66

Aa Bb Cc Dd Ee Ff Gg Hh Ii Jj Kk Ll Mm

magnet (magnets)
A magnet is a piece of iron or steel that has the power to pull other pieces of metal to it.

main
Main means the most important.

make (makes, making, made)
When you make something, you shape it or build it by putting several things together.

male
Any person or animal who can be a father is male.

mammal (mammals)
A mammal is an animal that can feed its young on milk.

man (men)
A man is a grown up boy.

manage (manages, managing, managed)
1. If you can manage to do something, you are able to do it, even though it might be difficult.
2. If you manage something, you look after it.
Mike was chosen to manage the hotel.

map (maps)
A map is a drawing of a place as it would look from above.
They used a map to find their way to the camp site.

march[1] (marches, marching, marched)
When you march, you walk like a soldier.

March[2]
March is the third month of the year. It has 31 days.

mare (mares)
A mare is a female horse.

mark (marks)
A mark is a spot or a line on something.
There was a mark on his face made in red ink.

market (markets)
A market is a place, usually in the open air, where things are bought and sold on stalls.

marmalade
Marmalade is a kind of jam made from oranges, lemons or limes.

marry (marries, marrying, married)
If two people marry, they become husband and wife.

67

Nn Oo Pp Qq Rr Ss Tt Uu Vv Ww Xx Yy Zz

mask (masks)
A mask is something that covers your face. It can be funny or it can be frightening.
Nobody recognised Justin underneath his mask.

match¹ (matches)
A match is a thin stick with a tip at the end that can be struck to make a flame.

match² (matches, matching, matched)
If two things match, they are alike in some way.
He wore a scarf which matched his hat.

68

material
Material is anything you need to make something.

matter (matters, mattered)
If something matters, it is important.
It doesn't matter if you fall over in the snow because it is soft.

mattress (mattresses)
A mattress is the soft thick part of the bed that you lie on.

may¹
May means perhaps.

May²
May is the fifth month of the year. It has 31 days.

meadow (meadows)
A meadow is a field full of grass.

meal (meals)
Breakfast, lunch and supper are all meals.

mean¹ (means, meaning, meant)
If you ask someone what they mean, you want something explained to you.

mean² (meaner, meanest)
If someone is mean, they are selfish and unkind.
He was too mean to share his sweets.

measles
Measles is an illness which gives you a high fever and small itchy red spots.

measure (measures, measuring, measured)
If you measure something, you find out how big or heavy it is.

meat
Meat is food which comes from animals.

Aa Bb Cc Dd Ee Ff Gg Hh Ii Jj Kk Ll Mm

medicine
Medicine is a liquid or tablets that the doctor gives you to make you feel better when you are ill.

medium
Medium is in between or halfway between two things.
He was of medium height — neither tall nor short.

meet (meets, meeting, met)
When people meet, they come together in the same place.

melt (melts, melting, melted)
If something melts, it turns to liquid when it is heated.
The ice melted in the hot sun.

men See man

mend (mends, mending, mended)
If you mend something, you put it back together when it has been broken.

mess
If things are in a mess, they are untidy and out of order.
I was in such a hurry to go out that I left the place in a mess.

message (messages)
A message is words that you leave for someone when you cannot speak to them.

messy (messier, messiest)
Something messy is not tidy.

met See meet

metal (metals)
Metal is a hard material like iron or steel.

metre (metres)
A metre is a measure of length. There are 100 centimetres in a metre.

mice See mouse

microwave (microwaves)
A microwave is a special oven that cooks food very quickly.

middle
The middle of something is halfway between the beginning and the end, or halfway between the top and the bottom.

midnight
Midnight is 12 o'clock at night.

mile (miles)
A mile is a measure of distance. It is equal to 1.6 kilometres.

milk
Milk is a white liquid that mothers give their babies to drink.

69

Nn Oo Pp Qq Rr Ss Tt Uu Vv Ww Xx Yy Zz

mill (mills)
A mill is a building where grain is crushed to make flour.

million (millions)
A million is the number 1,000,000.
A million is a thousand thousands.

mind¹ (minds)
Your mind is the part of your body that you use to think, feel and understand.

mind² (minds, minding, minded)
If you mind about something, you care about it.
I don't mind which programme we watch on television.

70

mine (mines)
A mine is a place underground where people work to dig out coal, jewels, salt or metals.

minute (minutes)
A minute is a measure of time. It is 60 seconds. There are 60 minutes in one hour.

mirror (mirrors)
A mirror is a flat piece of glass in which you can see yourself.
Mary smiled at herself in the mirror.

miss (misses, missing, missed)
1. If you miss someone, you are sad because they are not with you and you would like to see them.
2. If you miss a ball, you do not catch it.
3. If you miss a bus, you are not in time to catch it.

missing
If someone is missing, they are not where they should be.

mistake (mistakes)
If you make a mistake, you do something wrong, often by accident.
It was a mistake to go out without my umbrella because it poured with rain.

mix (mixes, mixing, mixed)
When you mix things, you stir or shake two or more things together.

mixture (mixtures)
A mixture is two or more things shaken or stirred together.

model (models)
A model is a copy of something like a boat or an aeroplane. It is usually smaller than the real thing.

modern
Modern means everything that is to do with life around you now.

Aa Bb Cc Dd Ee Ff Gg Hh Ii Jj Kk Ll Mm

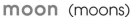

M

mole (moles)
A mole is a small animal that lives underground. It has tiny eyes and short dark fur.

moment (moments)
A moment is a very short time.

Monday
Monday is the day after Sunday and before Tuesday.

money
Money is the coins and pieces of paper used when people buy and sell things.
Alex had enough money to buy a new pair of shoes.

monkey (monkeys)
A monkey is a small lively animal with a long tail. Monkeys live in hot countries.

month (months)
A month is a period of time. It is about four weeks long. There are twelve months in a year.

monster (monsters)
A monster is a huge terrifying creature that you read about in stories.

moon (moons)
The moon is an object in the sky that goes around the Earth once every four weeks. The moon shines at night.

morning (mornings)
The morning is the first part of the day from sunrise until midday.

moth (moths)
A moth is an insect with wings. Moths usually fly at night.

mother (mothers)
A mother is a woman with a child or children of her own.

motor (motors)
A motor is the part inside a machine that makes it work.

71

motorbike (motorbikes)
A motorbike is a large bicycle with an engine.

motorway (motorways)
A motorway is a road with several lanes. They are built so that traffic can move quickly over long distances keeping away from the middle of towns and cities.

Nn Oo Pp Qq Rr Ss Tt Uu Vv Ww Xx Yy Zz

mount (mounts, mounting, mounted)
If you mount something like a horse, you get on its back.

mountain (mountains)
A mountain is a very high hill. It is often steep and difficult to climb.
The climbers had ropes and safety equipment with them to climb the mountain.

mouse (mice)
A mouse is a tiny animal with sharp teeth, whiskers and a long tail.

72

mouth (mouths)
Your mouth is the opening in your face that you speak and eat with.

move (moves, moving, moved)
When you move, you go from one place to another.

movie (movies)
A movie is a name for a film.

mud
Mud is a wet and sticky mixture of earth and water.

mug (mugs)
A mug is a large cup with a handle.

multiply (multiplies, multiplying, multiplied)
If you multiply something like a number, you make it larger.

munch (munches, munching, munched)
If you munch something, you chew it noisily.

muscle (muscles)
Your muscles are the parts inside your body that tighten and relax to make it move.
Nick's muscles ached after the long walk uphill.

museum (museums)
A museum is a place where interesting collections of things are on show for people to look at.

mushroom (mushrooms)
A mushroom is a small plant that looks like a little umbrella. Many types of mushroom can be eaten.

music
Music is made up of sounds that people sing or play on instruments.

mysterious
Something mysterious is strange and cannot be explained.

mystery (mysteries)
A mystery is something strange and puzzling that has happened.

Aa Bb Cc Dd Ee Ff Gg Hh Ii Jj Kk Ll Mm

nail (nails)
1. A nail is a short metal pin that you hammer into a piece of wood to hold it to another piece.
2. Your nails are the thin hard parts that cover the ends of your fingers and toes.

name (names)
Your name is what you are called.
My birthday card had a big badge on the front with my name on it.

narrow (narrower, narrowest)
If something like a road is narrow, it is thin not wide.
The road was so narrow that we had to reverse to let another car go by.

nasty (nastier, nastiest)
Someone or something that is nasty is very unpleasant.

natural
1. Something that is natural has not been made by people or machines.
2. Natural things have not been changed in any way.
Jo's front door was bright red, but Nancy's was still the natural colour of wood.

nature
1. Nature is everything in the world that has not been made by people.
2. Your nature is what you are like.

naughty (naughtier, naughtiest)
If you are naughty, you behave badly.

near (nearer, nearest)
If something is near, it is not far away.
The shops are so near that we can walk there in two minutes.

nearly
If you nearly do something, you almost do it, but not quite.
Jonathan nearly fell off his bike when he rode over a bump in the road.

neck
(necks)
Your neck is the part of your body that joins your head to your shoulders.
The giraffe stretched his long neck.

need (needs, needing, needed)
If you need something, you cannot manage without it.

needle (needles)
A needle is a thin pointed piece of metal with a hole in one end for putting thread through. Needles are used for sewing.

neighbour (neighbours)
Your neighbour is the person who lives next door to you.

74

nervous
A nervous person is easily frightened and worries a lot.
Bob was nervous about flying.

nest (nests)
A nest is a warm home for a young bird or other small animal.

net (nets)
A net is used for catching fish.

nettle (nettles)
A nettle is a plant which has leaves that sting.

new (newer, newest)
1. New things have just been bought or made.
Sophie wore her new shoes to school.
2. New things are different.

news
News is information about things that have just happened.

newspaper (newspapers)
A newspaper is several sheets of paper with information about what has happened in the world or in a certain area. Some newspapers are published each day and some are published each week.

nice (nicer, nicest)
1. You say something is nice when you like it.
2. If you are nice to people, you are kind to them.

night (nights)
Night is the time between sunset and sunrise when it is dark and most people and many animals are asleep.

nightdress
(nightdresses)
A nightdress is a loose long dress that women and girls sometimes wear in bed.

Aa Bb Cc Dd Ee Ff Gg Hh Ii Jj Kk Ll Mm

nightmare (nightmares)
A nightmare is a frightening dream.
Matthew had such a bad nightmare
that he woke up shouting.

nine
Nine is the number 9.

nod (nods, nodding, nodded)
When you nod, you move your
head up and down quickly to show
that you agree with something.

noise (noises)
A noise is a sound. It is often loud.
The children were making such a lot of
noise in the classroom that no one
could hear the bell.

noisy (noisier, noisiest)
If it is noisy, there is a lot of loud
noise.

nonsense
Nonsense is something that
does not make sense.
He was so tired that he spoke
complete nonsense.

north
North is one of the four main
compass points.

nose (noses)
You breathe and
smell with your
nose.

note (notes)
1. A note is a short
message.
2. A note is
a sound
in music.

notice[1] (notices)
A notice is a sign which gives you
information.
The notice said 'The show starts at
7.30 pm'.

notice[2] (notices, noticing,
noticed)
If you notice something, you see it,
hear it or smell it for the first time.

November
November is the eleventh month of
the year. It has 30 days.

number (numbers)
A number tells you how
many there are
of something.
There are 3
cakes and 5
sandwiches.

nurse (nurses)
A nurse is a person whose job it is to
look after people when they are ill in
hospital.

nut (nuts)
A nut is the hard fruit found on some
trees. You have to take the shell off
before you can eat it.

75

Nn Oo Pp Qq Rr Ss Tt Uu Vv Ww Xx Yy Zz

O

oak (oaks)
An oak is a large tree. It grows from an acorn and it loses its leaves in winter.

oar (oars)
An oar is a long pole with one flat end. You use oars to row a boat.

oasis (oases)
An oasis is a place in the desert where there is water and where trees grow.
At last they saw the trees and knew that they were near an oasis.

76

oat (oats)
Oats are the grains of a plant grown by farmers. Oats can be used to make food like porridge.

obey (obeys, obeying, obeyed)
If you obey someone, you do what they tell you to do.

ocean (oceans)
An ocean is a very big sea.

October
October is the tenth month of the year. It has 31 days.

octopus (octopuses)
An octopus is a sea creature which has eight arms.

odd (odder, oddest)
1. Something odd is strange.
2. An odd number cannot be shared equally: 3 is an odd number.

offer (offers, offering, offered)
1. If you offer something, you ask someone if they would like it.
2. If you offer to do something, you do it without being asked.

often
If something happens often, it happens many times.

oil (oils)
1. Oil is a thick smooth liquid that is used to keep engines running smoothly.
2. Oil is made from plants and can be used for cooking or for making dressings.

Aa Bb Cc Dd Ee Ff Gg Hh Ii Jj Kk Ll Mm

old (older, oldest)
1. A person or animal that is old has lived for a long time.
2. Something that is old has been there for a long time.
The church is very old. It was built 500 years ago.

olive (olives)
An olive is a small green or black fruit with a stone in the centre. Olives can be pressed to make oil and they can also be eaten.

one
One is the number 1.

open[1] (opens, opening, opened)
If you open something like a door, you move it so that people or things can go through it.

open[2]
If something is open, it is not shut.
The shop was open all day Saturday.

opposite[1]
The opposite of something is completely different from it. Tall and short, fat and thin, happy and sad are all opposites.

opposite[2]
If something is opposite something else, it is on the other side.
My cottage is opposite a field of cows.

orange[1] (oranges)
An orange is a round juicy fruit with a thick orange skin.

orange[2]
Orange is the colour of an orange.

orchestra (orchestras)
An orchestra is a large group of people playing musical instruments together.

order[1]
Order is the way things are arranged.
The dictionary is in alphabetical order: the words are arranged from A to Z.

order[2] (orders, ordering, ordered)
1. If you order something to eat or drink, you ask for what you want.
2. If someone orders you to do something, you must do it.

ordinary
Ordinary things are not unusual. You can see ordinary things all the time.

otter (otters)
An otter is a rare animal that lives near water. It has short brown fur, a long tail and webbed feet.

77

out
1. If you go out of a place, you are not there any more.
2. If a fire is out, it has stopped burning.

outside
1. The outside of something is the surface or the edges of it.
2. If you are outside, you are in the open air.

oven (ovens)
An oven is a space inside a cooker where you bake or roast food.

78

owe (owes, owing, owed)
If you owe money to someone, you have not paid them yet.
Angie owed Marie 50p, but she gave it back the next day.

owl (owls)
An owl is a bird that hunts at night. It has a flat face and large eyes.

own¹ (owns, owning, owned)
If you own something, it belongs to you.

own²
If you are on your own, you are alone.

pack (packs, packing, packed)
If you pack something like a box or a suitcase, you put things into it to take them somewhere else.

packet (packets)
A packet is a small parcel.

page (pages)
A page is one side of paper in a book or on a pad.

paid See **pay**

pain (pains)
A pain is the feeling you have when part of your body hurts.
I had a pain in my knee after I fell over.

paint¹ (paints)
Paint is a coloured liquid that you put on a surface with a brush, a roller or your hands.

paint² (paints, painting, painted)
If you paint something, you use a brush, a roller or your hands to put coloured liquid on it.

Aa Bb Cc Dd Ee Ff Gg Hh Ii Jj Kk Ll Mm

P

painting (paintings)
A painting is a picture that someone has painted.

pair (pairs)
A pair of things is two of them that belong together.
I lost one of my gloves so I had to buy a new pair.

palace (palaces)
A palace is a large building where a king, queen, prince, princess or bishop lives.

pale (paler, palest)
Something that is pale is a very light colour.
Her face went pale when she saw the accident.

palm (palms)
1. The palm of your hand is the inside of it between your fingers and your wrist.
2. A palm is a type of tree with big leaves that grows in hot countries.

pan (pans)
A pan is a wide pot for cooking.

pane (panes)
A pane is a sheet of glass in a window.

panic
Panic is a sudden feeling of fear that you cannot control.
There was panic in the zoo when the lion escaped.

pant (pants, panting, panted)
When you pant, you take lots of short breaths.

pantomime (pantomimes)
A pantomime is a play which tells a fairy story. The actors wear costumes and make the audience join in with songs and jokes.

paper
Paper is the material that you write and draw on or wrap things with.

79

parade (parades)
A parade is a long line of people walking through the streets.
We joined in the midsummer parade as it went through the village.

parcel (parcels)
A parcel is something wrapped up in paper ready to be posted or given as a present.

parent (parents)
A mother or a father is a parent.

park[1] (parks)
A park is an open space in a town with grass, trees and other plants, where people can go to walk, sit or play.

Nn Oo Pp Qq Rr Ss Tt Uu Vv Ww Xx Yy Zz

park² (parks, parking, parked)
When people park a car, they leave it somewhere while they go away from it for a time.
The town was so busy that we could not find anywhere to park the car.

parrot (parrots)
A parrot is a tropical bird with brightly-coloured feathers.

part (parts)
A part of something is a piece that belongs to something bigger.
My arms are parts of my body.

party (parties)
When you have a party, you ask your friends to come and share a special occasion with you.

pass (passes, passing, passed)
1. When you pass someone or something, you go by them.
2. If you pass a test, you are successful.
3. If you pass a ball to another player in a game, you give it to them.

passenger (passengers)
A passenger is someone who travels on a train or a boat or in an aeroplane or a car.

past
The past is time gone by.

pasta
Pasta is a food made from flour and water. It is the main food eaten in Italy. It is usually served with a sauce.

paste (pastes)
Paste is a thick wet mixture used to stick things together.

pastry (pastries)
Pastry is a mixture of flour, fat and water which is rolled flat and baked. Pastry is used to make tarts, flans and pies.

patient¹ (patients)
A patient is a person who is looked after by a nurse or doctor at home or in hospital.

patient²
If you are patient, you wait for something without getting cross.

path (paths)
A path is a narrow way through somewhere.

patrol (patrols, patrolling, patrolled)
When a group of people like the police patrol an area, they walk around it to see that there is no danger.

pattern (patterns)
A pattern is the way shapes and colours are arranged.

80

Aa Bb Cc Dd Ee Ff Gg Hh Ii Jj Kk Ll Mm

pause (pauses, pausing, paused)
If you pause, you stop for a very short time.

paw (paws)
A paw is the foot of an animal. It has soft pads underneath it and claws on each toe.

pay (pays, paying, paid)
When a person pays someone, they give them money in return for work or for something that they buy.
My mother paid the window cleaner once a month.

pea (peas)
A pea is a small round seed which grows in a pod. Peas are eaten as vegetables.

peace
Peace is a feeling of quiet and calm.

peacock (peacocks)
A peacock is a large male bird with long brightly-coloured tail feathers which it can spread into a fan shape. The female bird is called a peahen.

pedal (pedals)
A pedal is the part of something that you press with your foot to make it work. A bicycle has pedals.

peel
Peel is the skin on some fruit and vegetables.
Sara took the peel off her orange before she ate it.

pen (pens)
A pen is used for writing in ink.

pencil (pencils)
A pencil is a thin wooden stick with a thinner black or coloured strip inside it. You use a pencil for writing or drawing.

penguin (penguins)
A penguin is a black and white bird that does not fly. It uses its wings for swimming. Penguins live in the Antarctic.

people See **person**

perch (perches)
A perch is a seat for a bird.

perform (performs, performing, performed)
When you perform, you do something in front of a group of people.

period (periods)
A period of time is a length of time.
There was a long period of silence before Jolene put her hand up with the answer to the question.

81

Nn Oo Pp Qq Rr Ss Tt Uu Vv Ww Xx Yy Zz

person (people)
A person is a man, woman or child.

pest (pests)
A pest is any person, animal or plant that causes a lot of trouble.

pet (pets)
A pet is an animal that you like and keep in your home.

petrol
Petrol is a liquid made from oil. It makes the engines of aeroplanes, lorries and cars work.

phone (phones)
Phone is short for telephone.

photo (photos)
A photo is a picture taken with a camera. Photo is short for photograph.

82

piano (pianos)
A piano is a large musical instrument. It has black and white keys which you press with your fingers to make musical notes.

pick (picks, picking, picked)
1. If you pick fruit or flowers, you take them from the place where they are growing.
I like to pick my own strawberries.
2. If you pick one thing from among several, you choose it.

picture (pictures)
A picture is a drawing, painting or photograph.

pie (pies)
A pie is made of pastry with meat, vegetables or fruit inside.

piece (pieces)
A piece of something is a bit of it.

pier (piers)
A pier is a long thin platform. One end is on the land and the rest goes out over the sea.

pig (pigs)
A pig is a farm animal with thick skin and a curly tail.

pigeon (pigeons)
A pigeon is a grey bird that lives in towns or in woods. Pigeons make long low cooing sounds.

pile (piles)
A pile of something is when a lot of things are built up on top of each other.
Helen left a huge pile of dirty clothes on the floor.

pill (pills)
A pill is a small round piece of medicine which you swallow whole to help make you feel better when you are ill.

Aa Bb Cc Dd Ee Ff Gg Hh Ii Jj Kk Ll Mm

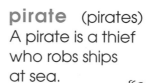

P

pillow (pillows)
A pillow is a soft cushion which you use to rest your head on in bed.

pin (pins)
A pin is a small sharp piece of metal with a point at one end and a flat head at the other. Pins are used to hold pieces of cloth or paper together.

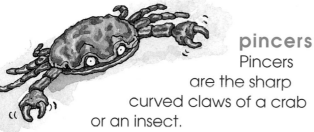

pincers
Pincers are the sharp curved claws of a crab or an insect.
Fred felt the sharp pincers of the crab as he put his toe into the rock pool.

pineapple
(pineapples)
A pineapple is a large fruit with a hard thorny skin that grows in hot countries. It is sweet and juicy.

pink (pinker, pinkest)
Pink is the colour you make when you mix red and white.

pipe (pipes)
1. A pipe is a long hollow tube that carries water, oil and other liquids from one place to another.
2. A pipe is something that people use for smoking tobacco.

pirate (pirates)
A pirate is a thief who robs ships at sea.

pizza (pizzas)
A pizza is a flat round piece of dough covered with tomatoes, cheese and other kinds of food, then baked in a very hot oven.

place (places)
A place can be a building, a town, a country or any particular area.

plain (plainer, plainest)
If something is plain, it is one colour and has no pattern on it.

plan (plans)
When you make a plan, you decide what you are going to do.
We made a plan of what to do on holiday.

plane (planes)
Plane is short for aeroplane.

planet (planets)
A planet is a large round object in space that moves round a star. The Earth is a planet.

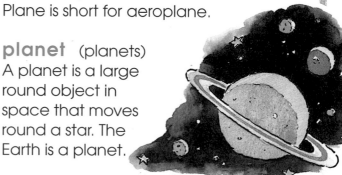

83

Nn Oo Pp Qq Rr Ss Tt Uu Vv Ww Xx Yy Zz

plant¹ (plants)
A plant is something that grows in the ground.

plant² (plants, planting, planted)
If you plant something, you put a seed, bulb or root into the earth so that it will grow.

plaster (plasters)
1. A plaster is a piece of sticky fabric that you use to cover a cut.
2. Plaster is a mixture that hardens when it dries. It is used to cover the inside walls of buildings.

plastic
Plastic is a light, strong, man-made material that is used to make many different things.

84

plate (plates)
A plate is a flat round dish for putting food on.

platform (platforms)
A platform is a part of a room that is higher than the rest.

play¹ (plays)
A play is a story that you act out. Sometimes you can use puppets.

play² (plays, playing, played)
1. When you play, you are in a game or you do something for fun.
2. When you play an instrument, you use it to make music.

playground (playgrounds)
A playground is a place where children can play.
There is a slide and a swing in the school playground.

playtime
Playtime is the time when you can have a break from school lessons.

pleasant (pleasanter, pleasantest)
Something that is pleasant is nice to listen to or to look at. Somebody who is pleasant is nice to be with.

please (pleases, pleasing, pleased)
If you please someone, you make them happy.

plenty
If there is plenty of something, there is more than enough of it.
There was plenty of food at the party.

plough (ploughs, ploughing, ploughed) (rhymes with cow)
If the farmer ploughs a field, he uses a machine to break up the earth.

plump (plumper, plumpest)
A person or animal that is plump is rather fat.

Aa Bb Cc Dd Ee Ff Gg Hh Ii Jj Kk Ll Mm

pocket (pockets)
A pocket is like a bag sewn into some clothes. You can keep small things like money or a handkerchief in your pocket.

pod (pods)
A pod is a case that holds the seeds of some plants. Peas and beans grow in pods.

poem (poems)
A poem is a short piece of writing which uses words in a special way. Poems often rhyme.

point[1] (points)
The point is the sharp end of something like a pen or a needle.

point[2] (points, pointing, pointed)
If you point at something, you hold out your finger towards it to show where it is.

poisonous
If something is poisonous, it could kill you or make you very ill if you ate it.

pole (poles)
A pole is a long strong stick of wood or metal.

police
The police are the men and women whose job it is to stop people from breaking the laws of the country.

polish (polishes, polishing, polished)
When you polish something, you rub it with a cloth to make it shine.

polite
Someone who is polite is well-behaved and speaks nicely.
My mother told me to be polite when we met the judge.

pond (ponds)
A pond is a small lake.

pony (ponies)
A pony is a small horse.

pool (pools)
A pool Is an enclosed area of water that can be natural or man-made.

85

poor (poorer, poorest)
1. People who are poor do not have much money.
2. You say someone is poor when you feel sorry for them.
Poor Charlie – he has the 'flu!

popular
Popular things or people are liked by everyone.
Computer games are very popular at the moment.

porridge
Porridge is a hot food made with oats and milk or water.

Nn Oo Pp Qq Rr Ss Tt Uu Vv Ww Xx Yy Zz

possible
If something is possible, it can happen or be done.

post¹
1. Post is the letters that the postman delivers to you each day.
2. (posts) A post is a strong pole fixed in the ground.

post² (posts, posting, posted)
When you post a letter or a parcel, you send it to someone by post.

poster (posters)
A poster is a large notice for people to read.
The poster said that the fair would be next Saturday starting at 2pm on the playing field.

postman (postmen)
A postman is a person whose job it is to deliver the post.

potato (potatoes)
A potato is a vegetable that grows under the ground. You cook it by boiling, frying or baking.

pour (pours, pouring, poured)
1. If you pour a liquid, you tip it out of a container.
2. If the rain pours, it falls very heavily.
The rain poured down for hour after hour, flooding the garden.

powder (powders)
Powder is something made up of very tiny pieces, like dust or flour.

power
Power is the strength that something or someone has.

practise (practises, practising, practised)
If you practise something, you do it over and over again to get better at it.

pram (prams)
A pram is a little bed on wheels for a baby.

pray (prays, praying, prayed)
If you pray, you talk to God.

present (presents)
A present is something that you give to someone.
Mandy wanted a model garage for her birthday present.

president (presidents)
A president is someone who is chosen to rule a country.

press (presses, pressing, pressed)
If you press something, you push hard on it.

86

Aa Bb Cc Dd Ee Ff Gg Hh Ii Jj Kk Ll Mm

pretend (pretends, pretending, pretended)
When you pretend, you act as if something is true when it is not.

pretty
Pretty things or people are pleasing to look at.

prey
Prey is any creature hunted by another creature.
The hawk swooped down on its prey.

price (prices)
The price of something is how much it costs.

prick (pricks, pricking, pricked)
If you prick something, you make a tiny hole in it with something sharp.

prince (princes)
A prince is the son of a king and queen.

princess (princesses)
A princess is the daughter of a king and queen.

print (prints, printing, printed)
1. When someone prints a book or a newspaper, they use a machine to do the writing and pictures so that they can make a lot of copies
2. When you print you write with big letters that are not joined together.

prison (prisons)
A prison is a place where people are kept as a punishment when they have done something against the law.

prize (prizes)
A prize is something that you win.

problem (problems)
A problem is something that is hard to understand or to answer.

programme (programmes)
A programme is something like a show on television or radio.

project (projects)
When you do a project at school, you find out as much as you can about something and then write about it.

promise (promises, promising, promised)
If you promise to do something, you mean that you will really do it.
I promised my mother I would do my homework before my friends came over.

proud (prouder, proudest)
If you are proud, you are very pleased because you have done something well.

87

Nn Oo Pp Qq Rr Ss Tt Uu Vv Ww Xx Yy Zz

public
If something is public, it is meant for everyone.

pudding (puddings)

A pudding is something sweet like an apple pie or a fudge cake that you eat at the end of a meal.

puddle (puddles)
A puddle is a very small pool of water. *Christine jumped in and out of the puddles with her red boots on.*

pull (pulls, pulling, pulled)
When you pull something, you get hold of it and make it come towards you.

puncture (punctures)
A puncture is a hole in a tyre.

punishment (punishments)
Punishment is something that is done to someone who has done something wrong.

pupil (pupils)
1. A pupil is someone who is taught something.
2. Your pupil is the black spot in the middle of your eye.

puppet (puppets)
A puppet is a kind of doll that you can move by using strings, rods or your hands.

puppy (puppies)
A puppy is a baby dog.

pure (purer, purest)
Something pure is clean and has nothing else mixed with it.

purple
Purple is the colour of grapes and plums. You can make purple by mixing red and blue together.

purse (purses)
A purse is a small bag for holding money.

push (pushes, pushing, pushed)
You push something when you press hard against it.

puzzle (puzzles)
1. A puzzle is a game or a question that is difficult to work out. You have to think about it to find the answer.
2. A puzzle is also a jigsaw puzzle.

pyjamas
Pyjamas are the loose shirt and trousers that some people sleep in.

88

Aa Bb Cc Dd Ee Ff Gg Hh Ii Jj Kk Ll Mm

quack (quacks)
A quack is the sound that ducks make.

quarrel (quarrels, quarrelling, quarrelled)
When people quarrel, they argue and speak angrily to each other.
My brothers always quarrel about whose turn it is to wash up.

quarry (quarries)
A quarry is a place where people cut out large pieces of stone.

queen (queens)
1. A queen is the woman ruler of a country.
2. A queen is the wife of a king.

question (questions)
A question is something you ask when you want to find something out.

queue (queues)
A queue is a line of people or vehicles waiting for something.
The queue stretched for five kilometres along the motorway.

quick (quicker, quickest)
If you are quick, you can do things very fast.

quiet (quieter, quietest)
If you are quiet, you do not make much noise.

quite
If something is quite good, it is good but not especially good.

quiz (quizzes)
A quiz is a game or a competition in which people try to answer a lot of questions.

89

rabbit (rabbits)
A rabbit is a small furry animal with long ears and a short tail. Rabbits live in holes in the ground.

race¹ (races)
A race is a competition to see who is the fastest.

race² (races, racing, raced)
If you race, you go as fast as you can to try to win the race.

rack (racks)
A rack is a shelf made of open bars where you can put things.

radiator (radiators)
A radiator is a metal heater for a room.

radio (radios)
A radio is a machine that receives sounds through the air. You can listen to programmes on a radio.

rag (rags)
A rag is an old piece of material.

90

railway (railways)
A railway is a track made up of two rails side by side for trains to run on.

rain (rains, raining, rained)
When it rains, little drops of water fall from the sky.

rainbow (rainbows)
A rainbow is a curved band of different colours that you can see in the sky when the sun shines through the rain.

rainforest (rainforests)
A rainforest is full of tall trees which grow in tropical countries where there is a lot of rain.

rake (rakes)
A rake is a tool with a long handle and spikes at one end. It is used for sweeping up leaves.

ran See run

rang See ring²

rare (rarer, rarest)
If something is rare, it is not often found.
The plant was so rare that the place where it grew was protected.

Aa Bb Cc Dd Ee Ff Gg Hh Ii Jj Kk Ll Mm

R

rat (rats)
A rat is a small animal with long sharp teeth. It has a scaly tail and looks like a large mouse.

rather
1. Rather means a little bit.
It was rather cold outside so I put on a warm jumper.
2. If you say you would rather do something else, you mean that you would prefer to do something else.

raw
Raw food is not cooked.

reach (reaches, reaching, reached)
If you reach a place, you get there.

read (reads, reading, read)
When you read something, you are able to say and understand words that are written down.
I can read my new book from beginning to end.

ready
If you are ready, you can do something immediately.

real
If something is real, it is not false.
Her hair is not a wig – it's real.

really
1. Really means very much.
I really wanted to pass my exams.
2. If you tell someone that something really happened, you want them to believe that you are telling the truth.

reason (reasons)
The reason for something is why it happens.

receive (receives, receiving, received)
If you receive something, it is given to you.

record[1] (records)
1. A record is a flat round piece of plastic that makes music when you play it on a record player.
2. A record is the best that has been done so far.

record[2] (records, recording, recorded)
If you record something, you write it down or put it on tape.
I decided to record the story that my granny told me because I thought my class would like to hear it too.

red (redder, reddest)
Red is the colour of ripe tomatoes.

reflection (reflections)
A reflection is what you see in a mirror or in water.

91

Nn Oo Pp Qq Rr Ss Tt Uu Vv Ww Xx Yy Zz

refrigerator (refrigerators)
A refrigerator is a metal cupboard which is kept very cold so that food stays fresh inside it.

refuse (refuses, refusing, refused)
If you refuse to do something, you say you will not do it.

religion (religions)
Religion is what people believe about a god or gods.

remember (remembers, remembering, remembered)
When you remember something, you still have it in your mind.
Can you remember what you had for lunch yesterday?

92

remind (reminds, reminding, reminded)
If you remind someone of something, you help them to remember it.

remove (removes, removing, removed)
If you remove something from somewhere, you take it away.

repair (repairs, repairing, repaired)
When you repair something, you mend it.

reply (replies, replying, replied)
When you reply, you give an answer.

reptile (reptiles)
A reptile is an animal with cold blood. Snakes and lizards are reptiles.

rescue (rescues, rescuing, rescued)
If a person rescues someone, they save them from danger.
The helicopter crew rescued a boy who had been washed out to sea.

rest¹
The rest is the part which is left.

rest² (rests, resting, rested)
If you rest, you stop what you are doing for a while.

restaurant (restaurants)
A restaurant is a place where people go to have a meal.

result (results)
A result is what happens because of other things.

reward (rewards)
A reward is a present that you get for doing something special.
The woman gave me a £5 reward for finding her cat.

Aa Bb Cc Dd Ee Ff Gg Hh Ii Jj Kk Ll Mm

rhinoceros (rhinoceroses)
A rhinoceros is a very large animal found in Asia and Africa. Rhinoceroses have horns on their noses.

rhyme (rhymes)
Words that rhyme end with the same sound as each other. Band and stand are examples of words that rhyme.

rhythm (rhythms)
Rhythm is a pattern of sound in poetry and music that is repeated.

rice
Rice is a white or brown food that is made from the seeds of a grass.

rich
If you are rich, you have a great deal of money.

ridden See **ride**²

riddle (riddles)
A riddle is a word puzzle.

ride¹ (rides)
A ride is a journey on an animal or a bicycle or in another vehicle.

ride² (rides, riding, rode, ridden)
If you ride a horse or a bicycle, you are on it while it is moving along.

rider (riders)
A rider is someone who rides something.

right
1. Right is correct or true.
2. Right is the opposite of left.

ring¹ (rings)
A ring is a circle of metal that you wear on your finger.

ring² (rings, ringing, rang, rung)
If you ring a bell, you make it sound.

ripe (riper, ripest)
If fruit is ripe, it is ready to eat.

93

rise (rises, rising, rose, risen)
When something rises, it goes up.

river (rivers)
A river is a lot of water that runs into a sea or a lake.

road (roads)
A road is a long hard piece of ground that takes traffic from one place to another.

Donkey Rides 50p

roam (roams, roaming, roamed)
If you roam, you wander about over a large area.

roar (roars, roaring, roared)
A roar is the loud deep sound that a lion makes.

roast (roasts, roasting, roasted)
If you roast something, you cook it slowly in the oven.
My dad decided to roast the chicken with garlic.

robin (robins)
A robin is a bird with a red breast.

robot (robots)
A robot is a machine that can move like a person. Robots are used in factories to do work which is boring for people to do.

rock¹ (rocks)
A rock is a large piece of stone.

rock² (rocks, rocking, rocked)
If you rock something, you make it move gently backwards and forwards.

rode See **ride**

roll (rolls, rolling, rolled)
If you roll, you turn over and over.

roof (roofs)
A roof is the covering for a house or other building.

room (rooms)
A room is one of the spaces inside a building. The kitchen, dining room and bedroom are all rooms.

root (roots)
A root of a plant is the part that grows underground.

rope (ropes)
Rope is made from very thick strong pieces of string or wire which are twisted together.

rose¹ (roses)
A rose is a flower with a sweet smell. Most roses have thorns on their stems.

rose² See **rise**

rough (rougher, roughest)
1. Something that is rough is not smooth.
2. If the sea is rough, it has high waves.
3. If someone is rough, they are not gentle.

94

Aa Bb Cc Dd Ee Ff Gg Hh Ii Jj Kk Ll Mm

round (rounder, roundest)
Something round is shaped like a circle or a ball.

row[1] (rows)
A row is a line of people or things side by side.
The children stood in a row at the front of the classroom.

row[2] (rows, rowing, rowed)
When you row, you use oars to make a boat move.

royal
Royal means to do with the king and queen.

rubber
1. Rubber is a strong stretchy material that bends and bounces.
2. (rubbers) A rubber is a small piece of rubber that you use to rub out pencil mistakes.

rubbish
Rubbish is everything that you throw away.

ruby (rubies)
A ruby is a precious red jewel.

rude (ruder, rudest)
If you are rude, you are not well-behaved or polite.

rug (rugs)
A rug is a small carpet.

ruin (ruins)
A ruin is a building that is falling down and is almost destroyed.
All that was left of the farmhouse after the fire was a burnt ruin.

rule (rules)
A rule tells you what you can or cannot do.

ruler (rulers)
1. A ruler is a strip of plastic, wood or metal used for measuring and drawing straight lines.
2. A ruler is someone who is in charge of an area or a country.

run (runs, running, ran, run)
When you run, you use your legs to move very quickly.

rung See **ring**[2]

rush (rushes, rushing, rushed)
When you rush you hurry.

rustle (rustles)
If you hear a rustle, you hear a sound like the soft moving of dry leaves on the ground.

95

Nn Oo Pp Qq Rr Ss Tt Uu Vv Ww Xx Yy Zz

S

sack (sacks)
A sack is a large bag made of cloth, plastic or thick paper.
We used old potato sacks to have races with in the garden.

sad (sadder, saddest)
If you are sad, you are unhappy about something.

96

saddle (saddles)
A saddle is a seat for a horse's back or for a bicycle so that you can ride it comfortably.

safari (safaris)
A safari is a journey that a group of people make to watch, photograph or hunt wild animals.

safe¹ (safes)
A safe is a very strong metal box where money and valuable things can be kept.

safe² (safer, safest)
If you are safe, you are away from danger.
Ian hid behind the door until he knew he was safe.

said See **say**

sail¹ (sails)
A sail is a large piece of material fixed to the mast of a ship or boat. When the sail fills with wind, it makes the boat move along.

sail² (sails, sailing, sailed)
To sail is to travel in a boat.

salad (salads)
A salad is a mixture of vegetables that you eat cold.
My favourite salad is tomatoes, lettuce and cucumber.

salt
Salt is a white powder that is used to make food more tasty.

same
If two things are the same, they are exactly alike.
I didn't know which twin was which because they looked the same.

Aa Bb Cc Dd Ee Ff Gg Hh Ii Jj Kk Ll Mm

sand
Sand is very small grains of rock found on beaches and in deserts.

sandal (sandals)
A sandal is a shoe that is held on the foot by straps.

sandwich (sandwiches)
A sandwich is made from two pieces of bread with a filling in between.

sang See **sing**

sank See **sink**[2]

sari (saris)
A sari is a long piece of material which is wound around the body in a special way to make a type of dress. Many Asian women wear saris.

sat See **sit**

Saturday
Saturday is the day before Sunday and after Friday.

sauce (sauces)
A sauce is thick liquid that is often made from vegetables or fruit. It is usually served with food to add to the taste.

saucepan (saucepans)
A saucepan is a metal pot with a handle which is used for cooking. It often has a lid.

saucer (saucers)
A saucer is a small round dish that you stand a cup on.

sausage (sausages)
A sausage is a tube of skin filled with tiny pieces of bread and meat. Sausages can be grilled or fried.

save (saves, saving, saved)
1. If you save someone, you get them out of danger.
2. If you save money, you put some aside each week or month, instead of spending it.

97

saw[1] (saws)
A saw has a blade with sharp teeth on one side. You use a saw to cut wood.

saw[2] See **see**

say (says, saying, said)
If you say something, you use your voice to make words.

Nn Oo Pp Qq Rr Ss Tt Uu Vv Ww Xx Yy Zz

scale (scales)
A scale is one of the small thin discs that make up the skin of fish and reptiles.

scales
Scales are used to find out how heavy things are.

scarf (scarves)
A scarf is a long piece of material that you wear around your neck to keep warm.

98

scatter (scatters, scattering, scattered)
When you scatter something, you throw many small things over a wide area.
When Gran's necklace broke, the pearls scattered everywhere.

school (schools)
A school is a place where young people go to learn things.

scissors
Scissors are tools for cutting. They have two long blades that open and close.

score (scores, scoring, scored)
If you score, you get a goal or a point in a game.
Justin scored two goals for his team.

scratch (scratches, scratching, scratched)
To scratch is to move a sharp object over something and damage it. Nails and claws can scratch.

scream (screams, screaming, screamed)
If you scream, you cry out because you are frightened or hurt.

screen (screens)
A screen is a flat surface that can be used to show a film.

sea (seas)
The sea is a very large area of salt water.

seal (seals)
A seal is a large animal that lives partly on rocky coasts and partly in the sea.

search (searches, searching, searched)
When you search for something, you look very hard for it.
After searching for two hours we found the kitten in the attic.

Aa Bb Cc Dd Ee Ff Gg Hh Ii Jj Kk Ll Mm

season (seasons)
A season is one of the four parts of the year. They are spring, summer, autumn and winter.

seat (seats)
A seat is something to sit on.

seconds (seconds)
Seconds are a measure of time. There are 60 seconds in one minute.

secret (secrets)
A secret is something that you don't want anybody else to know about.

see (sees, seeing, saw, seen)
If you see something, you use your eyes to look at something.

seed (seeds)
A seed is the small hard part of a plant that grows when you put it into the ground.

seek (seeks, seeking, sought)
When you seek something, you try to find it.

seen See **see**

sell (sells, selling, sold)
When you sell something, you exchange it for money.
The lady in the flower shop sold Geraldine a beautiful bunch of flowers.

send (sends, sending, sent)
If you send something, you make it go somewhere, usually by post.

sense (senses)
Your senses are the power to see, feel, smell, taste and hear.

sensible
If you are sensible, you are good at knowing the right thing to do.

sent See **send**

September
September is the ninth month of the year. It has 30 days.

serve (serves, serving, served)
If someone serves you in a shop or in a restaurant, they help you to get what you want.

set[1] (sets)
A set is a group of things which belong together.

99

Nn Oo Pp Qq Rr Ss Tt Uu Vv Ww Xx Yy Zz

set² (sets, setting, set)
When something sets, it becomes harder.
The cat left paw marks in the cement before it had time to set.

seven
Seven is the number 7.

several
Several things are a few things.

sew (sews, sewing, sewed, sewn)
When you sew, you use a needle and thread to fix pieces of material together.

sex (sexes)
The sexes are the two groups that people and animals belong to. One group is male and the other is female.
We did not know the sex of the gerbils until they had babies. Then we knew that one must be female and one male.

shadow (shadows)
A shadow is a patch of darkness that is made when there is something in the way of the light.

shake (shakes, shaking, shook, shaken)
If you shake, your body moves quickly up and down or from side to side.

shallow (shallower, shallowest)
If water is shallow it is not deep.
Terri couldn't swim so she stayed in the shallow end of the pool.

shampoo (shampoos)
Shampoo is liquid soap that you use to wash your hair.

shape (shapes)
The shape of something is the way its outside edges look. A ball is a round shape; a box is a square shape.

share (shares, sharing, shared)
When you share something, you give some of what you have to someone else.

shark (sharks)
A shark is a large sea fish with very sharp teeth. Some sharks are very dangerous.

sharp (sharper, sharpest)
Something sharp has an edge or blades that can cut.

Aa Bb Cc Dd Ee Ff Gg Hh Ii Jj Kk Ll Mm

shave (shaves, shaving, shaved)
When a person shaves, they take away hair that they do not want with a razor.
Dad shaves every morning.

shed (sheds)
A shed is a small hut.

sheep (sheep)
A sheep is a farm animal with a thick woolly coat. Sheep are usually kept for their wool.

sheet (sheets)
A sheet is a large piece of cloth that people use to put on a bed.

shelf (shelves)
A shelf is a strong board fixed to a wall or inside a cupboard. Shelves are used for putting things on.

shell (shells)
1. A shell is something you find → on the beach.
2. A shell is the thin hard cover of an egg or a nut. Some small animals like snails have shells.

shelter (shelters)
A shelter is a place where people and animals can keep out of the wind and rain.
The rain was so heavy that the walkers had to find a shelter until it stopped.

shepherd (shepherds)
A shepherd is a person whose job it is to look after sheep.

shine (shines, shining, shone)
When something shines, it gives out a bright light.

shiny (shinier, shiniest)
Something shiny is very bright.

ship (ships)
A ship is a large boat that travels on the sea.

101

shirt (shirts)
A shirt is a piece of clothing for the top half of the body.

shiver (shivers, shivering, shivered)
When you shiver, you shake because you are cold or nervous.
Angus started to shiver when he got out of the water.

shoe (shoes)
Shoes are what you wear on your feet to keep them warm and dry.

shone
See **shine**

shook
See **shake**

Nn Oo Pp Qq Rr Ss Tt Uu Vv Ww Xx Yy Zz

shoot (shoots, shooting, shot)
If you shoot, you use a gun or a bow and arrow to hit a target.

shop (shops)
A shop is a place where you can buy things.

short (shorter, shortest)
1. A short time is not long.
2. A short distance is not far.
3. A short person is not tall.

shot See **shoot**

102

shoulder (shoulders)
Your shoulder is the part of your body between your neck and your arm.

shout (shouts, shouting, shouted)
If you shout, you call out very loudly.

show¹ (shows)
1. A show is something you go to watch like a play or a pantomime.
2. A show is also an exhibition.

show² (shows, showing, showed, shown)
If you show someone something, you let them look at it.
Bob showed me his model cars.

shower
(showers)
1. A shower is a jet of water usually in the bathroom. You stand beneath it to get washed.
2. A shower is a short light fall of rain.

shown See **show**

shut¹ (shuts, shutting, shut)
If you shut something like a door, you close it.

shut²
If a shop is shut, you cannot go in to buy things.

shy (shyer, shyest)
A shy person is afraid to meet people they do not know.

side (sides)
The side of something is the part between the front and the back.

sigh (sighs, sighing, sighed)
If you sigh, you breathe out slowly and heavily. People often sigh to show that they are sad.

sign¹ (signs)
A sign is a notice that tells you something, by using pictures or words.

Aa Bb Cc Dd Ee Ff Gg Hh Ii Jj Kk Ll Mm

sign[2] (signs, signing, signed)
When you sign something like a letter, you write your name on it.
Jane asked the writer to sign his photograph for her.

silence
If there is silence there is no sound at all.

silk (silks)
Silk is very fine soft cloth made from thread spun by silkworms.

silver
1. Silver is a shiny light metal that is made into jewellery. Some knives and forks are made from silver.
2. The word silver is used to describe silver-coloured things.

sing (sings, singing, sang, sung)
When you sing, you make music with your voice.

single
1. Single means the only one.
Julie is a single child.
2. Single also means unmarried.

sink[1] (sinks)
A sink is a bowl with taps for washing things in.

sink[2] (sinks, sinking, sank, sunk)
If something sinks, it goes to the bottom of the water.

sister (sisters)
Your sister is the girl or woman who has the same parents as you.

sit (sits, sitting, sat)
When you sit, you bend your knees and put your bottom on a seat.

site (sites)
A site is the ground where something will be built.

six
Six is the number 6.

size (sizes)
The size of something is how big or small it is.

skate (skates)
A skate is a boot that has a blade of metal fixed underneath it for sliding on ice.

skeleton (skeletons)
A skeleton is all the bones of a body.

skill (skills)
Skill is being able to do something well.
Brendan had great skill as a juggler.

Vn Oo Pp Qq Rr Ss Tt Uu Vv Ww Xx Yy Zz

skin (skins)
Skin covers the whole body of humans and animals.

skip (skips, skipping, skipped)
When you skip, you hop first on one leg and then on the other.

skirt (skirts)
A skirt is a piece of clothing for girls and women to wear. Skirts hang from the waist.

sky (skies)
The sky is the space above the Earth. The sun, moon and stars are in the sky.

sledge (sledges)
A sledge is used for travelling over snow. It has strips of metal or wood underneath so it will slide.
Stevie and Kay slid down the hill on their new sledge.

sleep (sleeps, sleeping, slept)
When you sleep, you close your eyes and rest yourself completely.

sleeve (sleeves)
A sleeve is the part of a coat or dress that covers the arm.

slept See **sleep**

slice (slices)
A slice of something is a piece of it that has been cut.

slide (slides)
A slide is a long slippery piece of metal that children go down in a playground.
Sangeeta likes to go down the slide head first.

slip (slips, slipping, slipped)
If you slip, you fall down on something slippery.

slipper (slippers)
A slipper is one of a pair of soft shoes that you wear in the house instead of shoes.

slippery
Something slippery is difficult to walk on or to take hold of.
The fish was wet and slippery and Dad dropped it back into the river.

slow (slower, slowest)
Slow things do not go fast. When you move slowly, you take more time than usual.

104

Aa Bb Cc Dd Ee Ff Gg Hh Ii Jj Kk Ll Mm

slug (slugs)
A slug is a small creature like a snail without a shell.

small (smaller, smallest)
Someone or something small is little.

smash (smashes, smashing, smashed)
If you smash something, it breaks into many tiny pieces.

smell (smells, smelling, smelt)
1. If you smell something, you use your nose to find out about it.
I could smell the roses as I went up to the front door.
2. If something smells, it gives off a smell.
That garlic smells strong!

smile (smiles, smiling, smiled)
When you smile, you make a wide shape with your lips to show you are happy.

smoke
Smoke is the cloud of blue-grey gas that floats up from a fire.

smooth (smoother, smoothest)
Something smooth is flat with no bumps in it.
Teresa's pet snake had skin that looked shiny and smooth.

snack (snacks)
A snack is a small meal that is quick to prepare.
I always have a snack when I get home from school.

snail (snails)
A snail is a small slow-moving creature with a shell on its back.

snake (snakes)
A snake is a long thin creature without legs. Some snakes are poisonous.

snap (snaps, snapping, snapped)
If you snap something, you break it suddenly.
The ruler snapped in half when I trod on it by accident.

sneeze (sneezes, sneezing, sneezed)
When you sneeze, you make a sudden noise as air rushes out of your nose. You sneeze when you have a cold or when you have a tickle in your nose.

snow
Snow is small white flakes of frozen water that fall from the sky when the weather is very cold.

Nn Oo Pp Qq Rr Ss Tt Uu Vv Ww Xx Yy Zz

soak (soaks, soaking, soaked)
If you soak something, you make it very wet.
Betty got the ink stain out of her skirt by soaking it in milk.

soap
We use soap to wash with. Soap is made from fats with added colour and perfumes.

sock (socks)
A sock is a warm covering for your foot. Socks come in pairs.

soft (softer, softest)
Soft is the opposite of hard.
The raspberries were too soft and squashy to eat.

106

soil
Soil is earth that plants grow in.

sold See **sell**

soldier (soldiers)
A soldier is a member of the army.

solemn
If someone is solemn, they are serious.

solid
Something that is solid is hard and does not easily change its shape.
The ice cream was frozen into a solid lump.

song (songs)
A song is a piece of music with words.

sore (sorer, sorest)
If part of your body is sore, it hurts.

sort[1] (sorts)
Sort means kind or type.
What sort of present would you like – a toy or a book?

sort[2] (sorts, sorting, sorted)
If you sort things, you put them into groups.

sought See **seek**

sound (sounds)
A sound is a noise you hear.

soup
Soup is a liquid food made from meat or vegetables and water.

sour
Something sour tastes bitter or sharp.

south
South is one of the four points of the compass.

Aa Bb Cc Dd Ee Ff Gg Hh Ii Jj Kk Ll Mm

space
1. Space is the empty area between objects.
Do you have space in your garden for a greenhouse?
2. Space is beyond the Earth, where the stars and planets are.

spade (spades)
A spade is a tool that you use in the garden to dig holes. It has a long handle and a short wide blade.

speak (speaks, speaking, spoke, spoken)
When you speak, you open your mouth and say something.

special
Special things are different in some way.

speed
Speed is how fast or how slowly something goes.

spell[1] (spells)
In stories a spell is a magic rhyme or recipe that makes impossible things happen.
The wizard said a spell and the teapot poured out a cup of tea!

spell[2] (spells, spelling, spelled or spelt)
When you spell a word, you say or write the letters of the word together in the right order.

spend (spends, spending, spent)
When you spend money, you use it to buy something that you want.

spider (spiders)
A spider is a small creature with eight legs. Most spiders spin webs to catch their prey.

spill (spills, spilling, spilled or spilt)
If you spill something like milk, you let it fall out of its container by mistake.

spin (spins, spinning, spun)
1. If you spin something, you turn it quickly round and round.
2. When you spin, you make thread by twisting long thin pieces of cotton or wool together very quickly.

spine (spines)
1. Your spine is your backbone.
2. A spine is a long prickle on an animal or on a plant.

spire (spires)
A spire is the tall pointed part on top of a church tower.

spiteful
Someone who is spiteful is unkind and tries to upset people.

107

Nn Oo Pp Qq Rr Ss Tt Uu Vv Ww Xx Yy Zz

splash (splashes, splashing, splashed)
If you splash, you make drops of liquid fly up in the air.

split (splits, splitting, split)
If something splits, it cracks apart.

spoil (spoils, spoiling, spoiled or spoilt)
If you spoil something, you do something to it so that it is not as good as it was before.
The carpet was spoilt when Chi spilt coffee on it.

spoke See **speak**

spoken See **speak**

spoon (spoons)
A spoon is a tool with a long handle and a shallow bowl at the end that you use for eating.

sport
Sport is a game like football, netball or tennis.

spot (spots)
A spot is a small mark on something.

spout (spouts)
A spout is the part of a kettle or teapot that helps you to pour easily.

spray (sprays, spraying, sprayed)
If you spray water, you make it send out a lot of tiny drops of liquid over a large area.

spring
Spring is the time of the year when flowers begin to grow. It is the season after winter and before summer.

spun See **spin**

square (squares)
A square is a shape with four straight sides that are all the same length.

squeak (squeaks, squeaking, squeaked)
If something squeaks, it makes a tiny high sound.
The rocking chair squeaked as it moved backwards and forwards.

squeeze (squeezes, squeezing, squeezed)
If you squeeze something, you press it between your hands or fingers.

squirrel (squirrels)
A squirrel is a small furry animal with a long bushy tail. It eats things like nuts and seeds and lives in a nest called a drey.

Aa Bb Cc Dd Ee Ff Gg Hh Ii Jj Kk Ll Mm

stable (stables)
A stable is a
building where horses are kept.

stair (stairs)
A stair is one of a set of steps.

stand (stands, standing, stood)
When you stand, you are upright on
your feet without moving.
There were no seats so we had to stand.

star (stars)
Stars are the tiny
specks of bright
light that you see
in the sky at
night.

stare (stares, staring, stared)
If you stare, you look at someone or
something without looking away.

start (starts, starting, started)
When something starts, it begins.

station (stations)
A station is a building where trains or
buses stop for passengers.
*We waited at the station for half an hour
before the bus came.*

stay (stays, staying, stayed)
If you stay in a place, you do not
move from there.

steal (steals, stealing, stole,
stolen)
If someone steals, they take
something that does not belong
to them.

steam
Steam is the hot
mist that rises up
from boiling
water.

steel
Steel is a strong
metal made of
iron.

109

steep (steeper, steepest)
If something like a hill is
steep, it is hard to climb.

stem (stems)
The stem of a plant
is the stalk. It holds
up the leaves, flowers
or fruit.

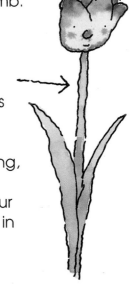

step (steps, stepping,
stepped)
If you step, you lift your
foot and put it down in
another place.

stick[1] (sticks)
A stick is a long thin piece of wood.

Nn Oo Pp Qq Rr Ss Tt Uu Vv Ww Xx Yy Zz

stick[2] (sticks, sticking, stuck)
If you stick two or more things together, you fix them together with glue or sellotape.

stiff (stiffer, stiffest)
If something is stiff, it is difficult to bend.

sting (stings, stinging, stung)
If something stings you, it gives you a sharp little stab of pain.

stir (stirs, stirring, stirred)
When you stir a liquid or a soft mixture, you move it around with something like a spoon.
Ailsa enjoyed stirring the cake mixture.

110

stole See steal

stolen See steal

stone (stones)
A stone is a small piece of rock.

stood See stand

stop (stops, stopping, stopped)
If you stop what you are doing, you do not do it anymore.

store (stores, storing, stored)
If you store things, you put them away for later.

storm (storms)
A storm is very heavy rain and strong wind.
The storm was so strong that it blew the roof off the house.

story (stories)
A story is words that tell you about something that has happened. Stories can be true or they can be made up.

straight (straighter, straightest)
Something straight has no bends in it.

strange (stranger, strangest)
Something that is strange is different, unusual or surprising.

straw (straws)
1. Straw is dry stalks of corn.
2. A straw is a thin tube that you use to drink through.

stream (streams)
A stream is a small river.

street (streets)
A street is a road in a town with houses or shops on both sides.

Aa Bb Cc Dd Ee Ff Gg Hh Ii Jj Kk Ll Mm

strength
Strength is how strong someone or something is.
The elephant had enough strength to pull up trees.

stretch (stretches, stretching, stretched)
When you stretch, you make yourself as long as you can.

strict (stricter, strictest)
If someone is strict, they expect you to do exactly what they tell you to do.
The teacher was very strict and would not let us talk at all.

string
String is very thin rope.

strip (strips)
A strip of something is a long thin piece of it.

stripe (stripes)
A stripe is a straight band of colour across something.

stroll (strolls, strolling, strolled)
If you stroll, you walk in a relaxed way and enjoy what you see.
That afternoon we strolled along the beach.

strong (stronger, strongest)
If you are strong, you can carry heavy things.

stuck See **stick**[2]

study (studies, studying, studied)
When you study, you spend time learning about something.

stung See **sting**

submarine (submarines)
A submarine is a boat that can travel under water.

111

suck (sucks, sucking, sucked)
It you suck something, you draw in liquid or air from it with your mouth.
The baby sucked the bottle until all the milk had gone.

sudden
If something is sudden, it happens when you do not expect it.

sugar
Sugar is something that you put in food to sweeten it. Sugar comes from a plant called sugar cane.

suit (suits)
A suit is a set of clothes with a top and bottom that match.

sum (sums)
A sum is a problem to be worked out using numbers.

summer
Summer is the season after spring and before autumn. It is usually the warmest time of the year.

sun
The sun is the bright star in the sky that gives the earth heat and light.

Sunday
Sunday is the day after Saturday and before Monday.

sung See **sing**

sunk See **sink**[2]

sunny (sunnier, sunniest)
When it is sunny, the sun is shining.

super
Super means extra special.
Muhammad took us for a drive in his super new car.

supermarket (supermarkets)
A supermarket is a large shop where you can buy food and other things for the house.

supper
Supper is an early evening meal.

supply (supplies, supplying, supplied)
If you supply something, you give it to someone who wants it.

sure
If you are sure about something, you know it is true or right.

surface (surfaces)
The surface of something is the outside or top part of it.

surprise (surprises)
A surprise is something that happens when you are not expecting it.
I had a surprise when my mother walked in with a new puppy.

swam See **swim**

sweep (sweeps, sweeping, swept)
When you sweep something, you clean it with a brush.

sweet (sweets)
A sweet is a small piece of food with lots of sugar in it.
Dee's favourite sweets are fruit pastilles.

swept See **sweep**

112

Aa Bb Cc Dd Ee Ff Gg Hh Ii Jj Kk Ll Mm

swim (swims, swimming, swam, swum)
When you swim, you move yourself through water without touching the bottom.

swing[1] (swings)
A swing is a seat which hangs from posts or from a tree for people to play on.

swing[2] (swings, swinging, swung)
If something swings, it moves backwards and forwards from a point that is fixed.

switch (switches)
A switch is something you press or turn to make something start up.

swum See **swim**

swung See **swing**[2]

syrup
Syrup is a thick sweet liquid.

system (systems)
A system is a set of parts that work together as one thing.
The computer system had a printer, a keyboard and a monitor screen.

table (tables)
A table is a piece of furniture with a flat top for putting things on.

tadpole (tadpoles)
A tadpole is a baby frog.

tail (tails)
A tail grows at the end of an animal.

takeaway (takeaways)
A takeaway is a meal that you buy to eat at home or somewhere else.
We bought our supper at the pizza takeaway and ate it beside the river.

113

tale (tales)
A tale is a story.

talk (talks, talking, talked)
When you talk, you speak to other people.

tall (taller, tallest)
1. Someone or something that is tall is not short.
2. A tall building is very high.

Nn Oo Pp Qq Rr Ss Tt Uu Vv Ww Xx Yy Zz

tame (tamer, tamest)
If an animal is tame, it is not wild.
You can keep tame animals as pets.

tangle (tangles)
A tangle is a twisted muddle of things.

tap (taps)
A tap is a handle on the end of a pipe that you turn on and off to make water flow or to stop it flowing.
I couldn't turn the tap off and the water overflowed onto the floor.

tape (tapes)
A tape is a long magnetic strip that you use to record sounds or pictures.

tarmac
Tarmac is a thick sticky black liquid that goes hard when it cools. It is used to make roads.

taste (tastes, tasting, tasted)
When you taste something, you put it on your tongue to see what it is like.

taught See **teach**

tea
Tea is a drink made by pouring boiling water onto the dried leaves of the tea plant.

teach (teaches, teaching, taught)
1. If you teach someone something, you help them to remember information.
2. If you teach someone something, you show them how to do it.

teacher (teachers)
A teacher is a person whose job it is to teach.

team (teams)
A team is a number of people who work or play a sport together.
The netball team had a party to celebrate their win.

tee-shirt (tee-shirts)
A tee-shirt is a top made of soft comfortable material.

teeth See **tooth**

telephone (telephones)
You use a telephone to speak to people who are far away.

television (televisions)
A television is a machine that brings pictures and sound through the air by electricity.

tell (tells, telling, told)
If you tell someone something, you pass on a story or information.

Aa Bb Cc Dd Ee Ff Gg Hh Ii Jj Kk Ll Mm

ten
Ten is the number 10.

tent (tents)
A tent is a shelter made of canvas. You use a tent when you go camping.

term (terms)
A term is a period of time. The school year is made up of three terms.

terrible
If something is terrible, it is very very bad.

thank (thanks, thanking, thanked)
If you thank someone, you show them that you are pleased about something they have done for you.
We thanked the mayor for opening the show.

theatre (theatres)
A theatre is a building where you can see plays, listen to music or see other entertainment.

thick (thicker, thickest)
1. If something is thick, it is not thin.
The tree trunk was so thick that Peter couldn't get his arms around it.
2. If a liquid is thick, it is not runny.

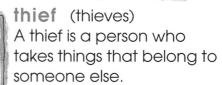

thief (thieves)
A thief is a person who takes things that belong to someone else.

thin (thinner, thinnest)
1. If a person is thin, they weigh less than most other people.
2. Something that is thin is not thick.
For Christmas my sister gave me a pen with a very thin nib.

115

thing (things)
A thing is anything that can be seen and touched. If you do not know what something is called, you say it is a thing.

think (thinks, thinking, thought)
When you think, you have words and ideas in your mind.
I tried to think of an idea, but nothing came into my mind.

thirsty (thirstier, thirstiest)
If you are thirsty, you need a drink.

thought See **think**

Nn Oo Pp Qq Rr Ss Tt Uu Vv Ww Xx Yy Zz

thousand
A thousand is the number 1,000.

thread (threads)
A thread is a thin piece of cotton, wool or nylon.

three
Three is the number 3.

threw See **throw**

throat (throats)
Your throat is the tube that takes the food from your mouth into your stomach.

through
If you go through something, you go from one side to the other.
Nigel went through the hedge to get the ball.

throw (throws, throwing, threw, thrown)
When you throw something like a ball, you send it into the air.

thumb (thumbs)
Your thumb is one of the five parts at the end of your hand. It is shorter than your fingers and is found at the side of your hand.

thunder
Thunder is a loud rumbling noise that follows a flash of lightning. You hear thunder when there is a storm.

Thursday
Thursday is the day after Wednesday and before Friday.

tidy (tidies, tidying, tidied)
If you tidy, you put things away in their proper place.
Andrew had to tidy up before he went to school.

tie[1] (ties)
A tie is a long narrow piece of cloth that is worn around the neck.

tie[2] (ties, tying, tied)
If you tie something, you fasten it with string or rope.

tiger (tigers)
A tiger is a large wild animal found in India and China. It has yellow and black striped fur.

tight (tighter, tightest)
Tight is not loose. Something that is tight fits very closely.

time
Time is what we measure in units of seconds, minutes, hours, days, weeks and so on. Time tells us when and how long something is.

116

Aa Bb Cc Dd Ee Ff Gg Hh Ii Jj Kk Ll Mn

tin

1. Tin is a silvery-white metal.
2. (tins)
A tin is a metal container which can be filled with food and sealed up.

tiny (tinier, tiniest)

Something or someone that is tiny is very small.

tired

When you are tired, you want to go to sleep.

toad (toads)

A toad is an amphibian that looks like a big frog. It has rough dry skin and lives in damp places on land.

toast

Toast is bread which is cooked until it is brown and crisp.

today

Today is the day that it is now. *Today is Sunday, yesterday was Saturday and tomorrow will be Monday.*

toe (toes)

Your toe is one of the short moving parts at the end of your feet. You have five toes on each foot.

told See **tell**

tomato (tomatoes)

A tomato is a round red fruit often eaten in salads.

tomorrow

Tomorrow is the day after today.

tongue (tongues)

Your tongue is the pink soft piece of flesh in your mouth. Your tongue helps you to taste, to eat and to speak.

tool (tools)

A tool is something you use to help you do something. Knives, spades and screwdrivers are all examples of tools.

tooth (teeth)

A tooth is one of the hard white objects that grow in your mouth. *Sheila's tooth fell out and she put it under the pillow for the tooth fairy!*

top (tops)

The top of something is the highest part of it.

tortoise (tortoises)

A tortoise is a small animal with a shell that covers its body. It moves very slowly.

touch (touches, touching, touched)

If you touch something or someone, you feel them.

tough (tougher, toughest)
If food is tough, it is hard to chew.

tower (towers)
A tower is a tall narrow building.

town (towns)
A town is a place with a lot of streets and buildings where people live and work.

toy (toys)
A toy is something you play with. Teddies, games, dolls and model cars are all toys.

118

track (tracks)
A track is a path for people to walk or run along.

tractor (tractors)
A tractor is a farm machine that can pull heavy weights. It has very large wheels.

traffic
Traffic is cars, lorries, motorbikes, buses, bicycles and other things that travel on the road.
The traffic stood still until the lights changed.

train¹ (trains)
A train is carriages joined together and pulled by an engine. It carries people and things.

train² (trains, training, trained)
When you train a person or an animal to do something, you teach them exactly what to do.
Zoe trained her dog to fetch the paper from the front door mat.

trap (traps)
A trap is used for catching animals, insects or birds.

travel (travels, travelling, travelled)
When you travel, you go from one place to another.

treasure (treasures)
Treasure is gold, silver and other precious jewels.

tree (trees)
A tree is a large plant with a trunk. It has branches with leaves on it.

tremble (trembles, trembling, trembled)
If you tremble, you shiver because you are afraid of what is going to happen.
Vicki started to tremble when she heard footsteps behind her.

triangle (triangles)
A triangle is a flat shape with three sides and three corners.

Aa Bb Cc Dd Ee Ff Gg Hh Ii Jj Kk Ll Mm

trick (tricks)
A trick is a clever thing to do to
entertain people.

trot (trots, trotting, trotted)
When a horse or pony trots, it
moves faster than a walk.

trouble
Trouble is something
that makes people upset
or worried.

trousers
Trousers are a piece of clothing that
cover your legs and the lower part
of your body.

truck (trucks)
A truck is a kind of lorry.

true (truer, truest)
If something is true, it is correct.
I promise that what I told you is true.

trunk (trunks)
1. The trunk of a tree is the main part
that grows out of the ground.
2. An elephant's trunk is its nose.
3. A trunk is a large suitcase.

trust (trusts, trusting, trusted)
If you trust someone, you believe
that they will not lie to you and
that they will not let you
down.

tube (tubes)
A tube is a long hollow
object, such as a pipe.

tuck (tucks, tucking, tucked)
If you tuck something in, you tidy the
loose ends away.

Tuesday
Tuesday is the day after Monday
and before Wednesday.

tug-of-war
(tugs-of-war)
A tug-of-war is
a competition
between two teams. The team
members pull on a big rope to see
which team is the strongest.

tumble (tumbles, tumbling,
tumbled)
If you tumble, you fall over and over.

119

tunnel (tunnels)
A tunnel is a long hole under the
ground or through a hill for trains
and traffic to go through.

turn[1] (turns)
When it is your turn to do something,
it is your go.

turn[2] (turns, turning, turned)
When you turn, you move to face
a different way.

Nn Oo Pp Qq Rr Ss Tt Uu Vv Ww Xx Yy Zz

turnip (turnips)
A turnip is a round white vegetable that grows underground.

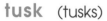

turtle (turtles)
A turtle is a large sea creature with a thick shell.

tusk (tusks)
Tusks are the long curved teeth that some animals have. Elephants and walruses have tusks.

twig (twigs)
A twig is a tiny branch.
The bird built its nest using tiny twigs.

twist (twists, twisting, twisted)
If you twist something, you turn or bend it to change its shape.

two
Two is the number 2.

tying See **tie**²

type (types)
A type of something is the sort that it is.

typewriter (typewriters)
A typewriter is a machine that has keys with letters of the alphabet on them. When you press a key, the typewriter prints a letter on paper.

tyre (tyres)
A tyre is a strong rubber ring filled with air that is fitted around a wheel.

120

ugly (uglier, ugliest)
Someone or something that is ugly is not pleasant to look at.

umbrella (umbrellas)
You use an umbrella to shelter from the rain.

uncle (uncles)
Your uncle is the brother of your father or mother.

underground
Underground is under the ground.

understand (understands, understanding, understood)
If you understand something, you know what it means.

Aa Bb Cc Dd Ee Ff Gg Hh Ii Jj Kk Ll Mm

uniform (uniforms)
Uniform is what people wear to show what job they do.
Mum wears a uniform when she goes to work – she's an air hostess.

upset (upsets, upsetting, upset)
When you upset someone, you make them unhappy.

upstairs
Upstairs is the top part of a house that you reach by a staircase.

urgent
If something is urgent, it is very important to do it straightaway.
Dee sent an urgent message for Sian to come home at once.

use (uses, using, used)
If you use something like a tool, you do something with it to help you.
Dan used his penknife to open the parcel.

useful
Useful things help you.

usual
Something that is usual happens often.

valley (valleys)
A valley is a low stretch of land between hills. A river often runs through a valley.

valuable
If something is valuable, it is worth a great deal of money or it is very important.

vampire (vampires)
A vampire is a creature in scary stories. Vampires have sharp pointed teeth called fangs.

van (vans)
A van is a covered truck for carrying things from place to place.

vegetable (vegetables)
A vegetable is a plant which is eaten raw or cooked. Potatoes, cabbage and beans are vegetables.

121

Nn Oo Pp Qq Rr Ss Tt Uu Vv Ww Xx Yy Zz

V

vehicle (vehicles)
A vehicle is anything that takes people and things from one place to another. Cars, vans, buses, carts and lorries are all vehicles.

velvet
Velvet is a soft material that feels furry on one side.

video (videos)
A video is a tape cassette used to record television programmes.

village (villages)
A village is a group of houses near each other often next to a church and some shops. Villages are usually in the country.

122

visit (visits, visiting, visited)
If you visit someone, you go to see them.

voice (voices)
Your voice is what you use to speak or sing.

volcano (volcanoes)
A volcano is a mountain with a crater at the top. Sometimes gases and hot liquid burst out of a volcano.

wagon (wagons)
A wagon is a farm cart with four wheels that a farmer uses to move heavy loads. It is often pulled by a horse or by oxen.

wail (wails, wailing, wailed)
If you wail, you let out a long sad cry because you are upset.

wait (waits, waiting, waited)
If you wait, you spend some time before anything happens.
Wait in the car while I go to the bank.

wake (wakes, waking, woke, woken)
If you wake, you stop being asleep.

walk (walks, walking, walked)
When you walk, you put one foot in front of the other to move along.

Aa Bb Cc Dd Ee Ff Gg Hh Ii Jj Kk Ll Mm

wall (walls)
1. A wall is used to divide two pieces of land from each other. It is usually made of brick or stone.
2. A wall is one of the sides of a room or building.

walrus (walruses)
A walrus is an animal that lives in the sea. It looks like a big seal. It has long tusks and a hairy face. Walruses usually come from the Arctic.

wand (wands)
A wand is a thin stick that is supposed to have magic power.

wander (wanders, wandering, wandered)
If you wander, you walk about without trying to go anywhere in particular.
Jamie wandered along the road, enjoying the sunshine.

want (wants, wanting, wanted)
When you want something, you wish for it or need it.
Billy wants a bike for his birthday.

war (wars)
War is a fight between countries that can go on for a long time.

wardrobe (wardrobes)
A wardrobe is a cupboard to keep your clothes in.

warm (warmer, warmest)
If something is warm, it is fairly hot.

warn (warns, warning, warned)
If you warn someone, you tell them that they are in danger.
Mum warned Ellie not to step on the ice because it was thin.

wash (washes, washing, washed)
When you wash, you use water and soap to clean yourself.

wasp (wasps)
A wasp is an insect like a bee. Wasps sometimes sting.

waste¹ (wastes)
Waste is whatever is no longer wanted.

waste² (wastes, wasting, wasted)
If you waste something, you use more than you need of it.
She wastes electricity by leaving all the lights on.

watch¹ (watches)
A watch is a small clock that you wear on your wrist.

123

Nn Oo Pp Qq Rr Ss Tt Uu Vv Ww Xx Yy Zz

watch² (watches, watching, watched)
When you watch something, you look at it to see what happens.
The walkers stopped to watch the buzzard soaring in the sky.

water
Water is a clear liquid that falls from the sky as rain and flows in rivers to the sea.

waterproof
Waterproof things keep out water.

124

wave (waves)
A wave is a line of water that moves on the sea.

wax
Wax is a hard material made of oil or fat. It becomes soft when it melts.
The candle wax burned slowly.

weak (weaker, weakest)
Someone or something that is weak does not have much strength.
Ben felt so weak that he could not lift the chair.

wear (wears, wearing, wore, worn)
When you are wearing clothes, you have them on.

weather
Weather is what it is like outside each day. Rain, snow, sun, fog and wind are all part of the weather.

web (webs)
A web is a thin net that spiders build to catch their prey.

Wednesday
Wednesday is the day after Tuesday and before Thursday.

weed (weeds)
A weed is a plant that grows where you do not want it to grow.

week (weeks)
A week is seven days. There are 52 weeks in a year.

weigh (weighs, weighing, weighed)
When you weigh someone or something, you find out how heavy they are.

weight (weights)
Weight is how heavy something is.

well¹ (wells)
A well is a deep hole in the ground which has been dug to reach water.

Aa Bb Cc Dd Ee Ff Gg Hh Ii Jj Kk Ll Mm

well [2]
If you are well, you are healthy.

west
West is one of the four main points of the compass. The sun sets in the west.

wet (wetter, wettest)
Wet is not dry. If something is wet, it is covered with liquid.

whale (whales)
A whale is the largest sea animal in the world.

whistle [1] (whistles)
A whistle is an object that makes a high-pitched sound when you blow through it.

whistle [2] (whistles, whistling, whistled)
When you whistle, you blow air through a tiny gap between your lips. It makes a high sharp sound.

white (whiter, whitest)
White is the colour of snow.

whole
The whole of something is all of it.

wide (wider, widest)
Something wide measures a large distance from side to side.
The river was so wide that it took the ferry half an hour to cross it.

125

wheat
Wheat is a plant grown on farms. Its seeds are used to make flour.

whisper (whispers, whispering, whispered)
If you whisper, you speak very quietly.
Bobby and Jo whispered at the back of the classroom so that their teacher would not hear them.

wild (wilder, wildest)
Wild animals live in fields, jungles and forests. They are not tame. Wild plants grow in fields and woods and are not looked after by people.

win (wins, winning, won)
If you win a race or a competition, you come first.

wind
Wind is the moving of air.

Nn Oo Pp Qq Rr Ss Tt Uu Vv Ww Xx Yy Zz

window (windows)
A window is a sheet of glass that covers a hole in the wall. Windows let in the light from outside.

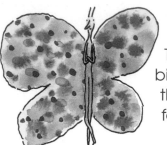

wing (wings)
The wings of a bird or insect are the parts they use for flying.

winter (winters)
Winter is the season that is after autumn and before spring. It is usually the coldest time of the year.

wire (wires)
Wire is a long thin strip of metal.
The bird cage was made of wire.

126

wise (wiser, wisest)
Someone who is wise knows a lot of things.

wish (wishes, wishing, wished)
If you wish that something would happen, you want it very much.

witch (witches)
A witch is a woman who uses magic. In fairy stories witches fly on broomsticks and wear long pointed hats.

wobble (wobbles, wobbling, wobbled)
If something wobbles, it shakes from side to side.
The jelly wobbled so much that it slid off the plate.

woke See **wake**

woken See **wake**

wolf (wolves)
A wolf is a wild animal like a large dog.

woman (women)
A woman is a girl who has grown into an adult.

won See **win**

wonder (wonders, wondering, wondered)
If you wonder about something, you are not sure about it and want to know more.
Danny wondered how the stars stayed up in the sky.

wood¹
Wood is the hard material from the trunks of trees.

wood² (woods)
A wood is a lot of trees growing together.

Aa Bb Cc Dd Ee Ff Gg Hh Ii Jj Kk Ll Mn

wool
Wool is the thick soft hair that grows on sheep. It can be used for making cloth or for knitting.

word   (words)
A word is a group of letters that means something when you write, say or read it.

wore   See **wear**

work   (works, working, worked)
When you work, you do a job.

world
The world is the planet we live on.

worm   (worms)
A worm is a long thin creature that lives in the soil.

worn   See **wear**

worry   (worries, worrying, worried)
If you worry, you keep on thinking about your problems.
Anna worried about her exams.

worth
If something is worth a particular amount of money, that is how much you would have to pay to buy it.

wound   (wounds)
A wound is a cut or a hole in someone's flesh.

wrap
(wraps, wrapping, wrapped)
When you wrap something, you put paper or cloth around it to protect it in some way.
The lady wrapped the fish and chips in white paper.

wriggle   (wriggles, wriggling, wriggled)
When you wriggle, you twist and turn your body very quickly.

wrinkle   (wrinkles)
A wrinkle is a small line in the skin.

127

wrist   (wrists)
Your wrist is the joint between your arm and your hand.

write   (writes, writing, wrote, written)
When you write, you put words on paper so that people can read them.
Jo wrote a funny poem.

wrong
If you are wrong, you are not right.

wrote   See **write**

Nn Oo Pp Qq Rr Ss Tt Uu Vv Ww Xx Yy Zz

X Z
Y
X

Xx

X-ray (X-rays)
An X-ray is a special photograph that shows the inside of the body.

xylophone (xylophones)
A xylophone is a musical instrument. It has wooden bars that you hit with a hammer.

year (years)
A year is twelve months.

yell (yells, yelling, yelled)
If you yell, you shout loudly.

yellow (yellower, yellowest)
Yellow is the colour of daffodils and sunshine.

yelp (yelps, yelping, yelped)
When a dog yelps, it makes a short loud cry.

young (younger, youngest)
Young things are not old. They have not lived very long.

128

yacht (yachts)
A yacht is a boat which has sails or a motor.

yard (yards)
A yard is a space outside a building. Yards are usually made of concrete and they have a wall or a fence around them.

yawn (yawns, yawning, yawned)
When you yawn, you open your mouth wide because you are tired.
At the end of the programme Dad yawned heavily and went off to bed.

zebra (zebras)
A zebra is an animal like a horse. It has black and white stripes and lives wild in Africa.

zip (zips)
A zip is a plastic or metal fastener on clothes and on other things. When you close the zip, the teeth on it join up tightly.

zoo (zoos)
A zoo is a park where animals are kept for people to study and watch.